One Nation Under God
The Triumph of the Native American Church

One Nation Under God

The Triumph of the Native American Church

Compiled and Edited by

HUSTON SMITH & REUBEN SNAKE

Walter B. Echo-Hawk, James Botsford, Jay C. Fikes,
Phil Cousineau, Gary Rhine, Edward Anderson,
and members of the Native American Church

Clear Light Publishers
Santa Fe, New Mexico

Clear Light Publishers
823 Don Diego, Santa Fe, New Mexico 87501
WEB: www.clearlightbooks.com

Paperback Edition
10 9 8 7 6 5 4 3 2 1

Library of Congress Cataloging-in-Publication Data

One nation under God : the triumph of the Native American Church/edit-ed by Reuben Snake and Huston Smith.

     p. cm.

    ISBN: 1-57416-006-0 $14.95

    1. Native American Church of North America. 2. Indians of
North America Religion. 3. Freedom of religion United
States. I. Snake, Reuben. II. Smith, Huston.

E98.R3053 1995

299'.7—dc20   95-33980

                                                   CIP

Printed in Canada

COVER ART: "White Buffalo," acrylic, by Bobby Hill, Kiowa. Courtesy Oklahoma Indian Arts Gallery.

Contents

Foreword

It is likely that few Americans are aware that a nation whose founders came to this continent to escape religious persecution later engaged in broad-scale effort to discourage the expression by the native people of this country of their religion, their culture, and their traditions. This government-initiated repression of those rights which are protected by the First Amendment to the United States Constitution was implemented through federal laws and regulations, and military directives which ordered soldiers to shoot on sight those Indian people found to be engaged in ghost dancing and other traditional manifestations of their cultures. Surviving women and children were rounded up and imprisoned. Indian children were punished for speaking their native languages in school settings, forbidden to wear their native dress or practice their native customs. When these efforts to eliminate all vestiges of the religion and culture and traditions of native people proved unsuccessful, Indian children were removed from their homes and sent either to boarding schools or to be raised in non-Indian homes, where they could be effectively separated from the influences of their parents and grandparents, their families and their tribal communities. Although these systematic attempts to destroy the cultures and religions of a native people became less visible over the years, they continued well into contemporary times. As recently as the 1960s, the goal of federal Indian policy was the forced "termination" of the official existence of all Indian tribes.

It is within this repressive climate and historical context that the struggles of the Native American Church and the unflagging efforts of one of its great leaders, Mr. Reuben Snake, must be understood.

Centuries before there was an environmental movement in the United States, the native people of this country expressed their reverence for the earth and all of its creatures on a daily basis. The conservation and preservation of natural resources were an unquestioned and integral part of everyday life. It is only in modern times that we as a nation have begun to realize how much we have to learn from the First Americans.

So too, I believe, will inspiration be found in the pages which follow.

Senator Daniel K. Inouye
Washington, D.C.

Preface

In a place apart, closer to nature than to the human scene, a tepee throws its outline against the night sky, a sacred silhouette. Inside, thirty or so Indians, men and women, sit on blankets and mats around a fire. Several children are sleeping in their parents' laps or on the ground by their sides. A seven-stone water drum pounds loudly and rapidly — the fetal heartbeat raised to cosmic proportions. Songs are sung with piercing intensity, interspersed with prayers and confessions. Tears flow, and a sacrament is ingested.

It is a congregation of the Native American Church, holding one of its appointed meetings.

The Native American Church (NAC) is the spiritual bulwark of a quarter million of the original inhabitants of this continent. Its roots extend into the twilight zone of prehistory, before the rise of Christianity or any of the historical religions. But because its sacrament is Peyote ("God's Flesh") whereas that of the dominant religion in the United States is alcohol ("Christ's Blood"), members of the Native American Church have had to worship under a cloud since European invaders took over. Its members could not practice their religion without fearing a knock on the door.

That fear escalated in the 1990s as a result of the Supreme Court's explicit ruling (on April 17, 1990, in *Employment Division of Oregon v. Smith*) that the Bill of Rights — specifically the "free exercise of religion" clause in the First Amendment to the United States Constitution — does not extend to the Native American Church because of its sacramental use of Peyote.

This book is the story of the Native Americans' response to — and victory over — that ruling. The judicial branch of the United States having deserted them, they resorted to its legislative branch. Without a nickel in their coffers, they challenged the highest court of the land on the Peyote issue and won, reversing (by four years of determined effort) four centuries of prejudice against their sacrament. It is a story that deserves to be documented, remembered, and retold for generations, for it carries hope for freedom lovers throughout the world.

The prime mover in securing the passage by Congress of the *American Indian Religious Freedom Act Amendments of 1994* (which President Clinton signed into Public Law 103–344 on October 6, 1994) was Reuben Snake, this book's co-editor. Originally, the book was intended, in partnership with a documentary film, *The Peyote Road*[1], to arouse public support for the Act just mentioned, but with its passage the book has turned into a profile of the oldest and most misunderstood religion in America: its history, structure, what it means to its

[1]A sixty-minute documentary film and videotape directed by Fidel Moreno, Gary Rhine, and Phil Cousineau (1992). Available from Kifaru Productions, 1550 California Street, San Francisco, CA 94109; telephone, (415) 381-6560.

adherents, and above all its landmark triumph over centuries of adversity.

Reuben Snake lived to see neither the passage of the Act he conceived nor the completion of this book, but on the book he had done enough to warrant retaining his name as co-editor. (The extraordinary events surrounding his death are reported in the Epilogue.) Though I must take responsibility for the book's final form, it could not have been completed without the support of Reuben's family and his stalwart friends, among whom the following deserve special mention: Walter Echo-Hawk, Johnny White Cloud, James Botsford, Jeffrey Bronfman, Phil Cousineau, Jay Fikes, Willard Johnson, and Gary Rhine. To all of these, and to Harmon Houghton, its publisher, Sara Held, its editor, and Howard Curtis, who caught a number of typographical errors, my sincerest thanks.

Huston Smith
Berkeley, California

The Beauty of NAC, *oil painting by Hayna Brown.*

Introduction

Reuben Snake

As the Native American Church has been at the center of my adult life, it is impossible for me to think of it impersonally. The natural way for me to introduce my Church, therefore, is to speak in my own voice as clearly and honestly as I can; not that I will be talking much about Reuben Snake, though I will refer to my ancestors as we indigenous peoples always do. After introducing myself I shall turn to our Church, yet indirectly I will still be speaking about myself, for the Church's beliefs and practices are the most important thing about me. They have structured my life, and I don't want them ever to climb out of me.

I am a Hochunk; other people refer to us as Winnebagos. My English name is Reuben Snake, but I also have an Indian name, *Kikawunga*, which means a great deal to me, for it is a very old, traditional name for my clan of the Winnebago people. On Easter Sunday morning, 1939, my grandmother's uncle, my great-grandfather, baptized me into the Native American Church and christened me *Kikawunga*, a name that is remarkable not only for its antiquity but for its connotations, for it means "To Rise Up." I was well into my adult life before I realized the connection between the meaning of that name and the day of the year — Easter Sunday — that I received it. I came to see that in giving me that name my great-grandfather was commissioning me to help resurrect the heritage of my people.

15

I have tried to fulfill that commission, particularly as it relates to the Native American Church. There is a great deal of chaos and confusion in today's world, but God's truth (as it comes to us through our Church) is eternal and always available to us. Human wisdom, though, is finite, so we begin to question God's truth and argue among ourselves. Our minds become like clouds that darken the sky and sometimes even black it out. Five centuries of oppression against Native Americans have abetted this confusion.

The elders of my race and tribe say that in the moment when the first human being became consciously aware of the creation — when he *saw* the creation, when he *heard* the creation, when he *felt* and *smelled* the creation — exercising all of his senses for the first time, he realized that he was in the midst of something great and wonderful, and that it could not have come into being by accident. It had to have had a Creator. It was then that he realized that he was himself a part of creation, and that he had to live up to his place in it. To do that, he had to tune his life to the rhythms and harmony of creation.

When our original ancestor came to this realization — that he had to bend his will, find his place within this creation, and live in peace and harmony with it — he knew that he had to put its Creator first in his life. Everything that he did had to be directed toward honoring and respecting the Great Spirit, the creator of all things. From that moment on, our original ancestor fashioned his life by that principle. This is the meaning of our ceremonial life. Everything we do — our music, our dancing, our rituals — is done to honor the Creator and find our place in his creation. This is the way our people see things. We try to live in peace and harmony with creation. It is our version of the Bible's injunction to "Seek ye first the kingdom of God and his righteousness (I emphasize *his* righteousness) and all things shall be added unto you."

This is the way our ancestors lived for countless generations. They put the Creator first, and we try to follow them in that. We try to respect and honor our families and friends; we try to have compassion for our fellow men, for that's what our Creator tells us to do. These truths are like the sunlight; they are always present. As long as we live by them, we are in tune with the Creator. In principle, we Indian people, all the days of our lives, seek the Creator's righteousness as the prerequisite for receiving from him in return. But this gets us into trouble with the larger society that surrounds us, because that society seems to have different standards for what is right and wrong.

My branch of the Native American Church has incorporated many Christian teachings, including the six days of creation followed by a seventh day for rest. But this is an overlay, superimposed on our original awareness that every day is a holy day. This is what my grandmother taught us while we were little. She taught us to get out of our beds every day before the sunrise, stand outside our lodges, and as the sun comes up over the horizon we should raise our hands to the Creator and thank him for the life that is ours that day. And we should ask forgiveness in advance for any way that we might disturb creation in the day that is beginning. We are going to need food. We are going to need warmth. We are going to need clothing. We are going to need all these material things that our bodies require, which means that we are going to have to take things from Grandmother Earth. We have to take the life of our brother the buffalo, or the elk, or the deer; so we should ask the Creator's forgiveness for things that we will be doing that might threaten the rhythm and harmony of nature that sustains us. These attitudes are the foundation of the red man's realization that every day is a sacred day, a holy day. For we are alive! We are breathing! We still have our senses, and are able to move about in the divine creation.

This brings me to an important point. The outlook I have been describing comes to us through a sacred herb, one that is sacred because it is, in fact, divine. We call it Peyote, but more often, because of what it does for us, we call it our Medicine.

My people have an old story about this herb. They talk about its power. They say that this particular herb is the most powerful of all the plants because God endowed it with his love and compassion. He put those qualities into this lowly herb so that when we eat it we can feel that the love that God is — I emphasize the love that God *is*, not that God *has* — is physically inside us. From there it overflows in compassion for human beings and all other kinds of creatures. It enables us to treat one another tenderly, and with joy, love, and respect.

For Native American Church members, this is our daily life. Each day we try to keep in mind the thoughts that I have mentioned. During the day, as we partake of the earthly blessings that we have been given, we thank the Creator and our Grandmother Earth. And when we go to bed at night we thank the Great Spirit for bringing us through the day that is ending and ask him to keep us safe through the night.

This is the teaching of the Native American Church, so it was the way I was raised. Around the tepee's holy fire my elders told me these things repeatedly, for they wanted me to understand. While we were children, boys and girls alike, we were included in the Church's rituals. Each of us was taught to perform certain parts of its ceremonies. We would go into the woods to find wood for the sacred fire, for example. Not any old wood would do; it had to be of the right sort to feed a fire that would reveal God's will to us. The flames of that fire would be God's tongue, talking to us. We knew by heart the legends that explained those things. I never tired of hearing the old people tell their stories because every time they did so they caused me to feel a special joy in the company of my people and our Creator.

This specificity regarding sacred firewood carries over into every aspect of our sacramental life. Each tribe has its distinctive way of erecting its tabernacle, its tepee and the altar within it. It is interesting that those specifications approximate the directions given to the tribes of Israel for constructing their tabernacles. At many points the two sets of instructions are parallel if not identical. This gives Indians insights into why the Israelites did what they did, and continue to do what they do. When God told the Israelites to construct their altars from the earth and to keep them on the earth — don't hew them from stone, and don't build steps up to them — we hear instructions that resemble those our ancestors were given. Our altars, too, are to be built on the earth and from earth, and we are to sit on the earth around them. Sitting on the ground tokens humility, and my name, Reuben Snake, makes me more conscious of that virtue than usual. Snakes are not the most exalted of creatures; they are earth-bound, they hug the earth. In playful moments I sometimes introduce myself as Reuben Snake, your humble serpent.

In addition to sitting on the ground around our altars, we encircle them. This too is significant, for in doing so we again conform to the patterns of nature. Stars circle, days become nights then days again, summer turns into winter then returns to summer — gyres and turnings are everywhere. As we surround the sacred fire with the circle of our bodies, we ingest the divine medicine which heals our souls. Keeping our minds on the fire, we raise our voices in prayer songs that bring our minds together, uniting them. We do this whatever the immediate purpose of the gathering. Our prayers could be for the healing of someone's sick body, or mind, or emotions, or to celebrate the birth of a child and wish it a long and happy life. One of our young people may be entering the armed forces and we want him to be safe. We want him to fulfill his military obligations honorably and come home to us healthy and in a good frame of mind. Whatever our immediate concerns happen to be, we voice them as we sit in our circle facing the sacred fire. Instead of looking at the neck of the person in front of us as in Christian churches, we look directly into God's face, his fire. In the prayer songs that bring our hearts together, we offer our single, united heart to the Great Spirit.

That is what Peyote is all about. Because it is interfused with God's love, it does good things for us. I've already spoken of some of the symbolism of its ritual, but there is more to relate. When we walk through the narrow entry to our tepee we are returning to the womb of our mother. And when we sit in the tepee we are in that womb. Being there, we are perfectly safe, which is a way of saying that we are the way God made us. Outside the tepee, in the everyday world, we hide behind defenses — psychological strategies that we use to cope with one another; the way we dress, the way we talk, mechanisms for impressing one another. These, though, are not God's doings. They are overlays that have to be peeled away if we are to experience the love that doesn't need them. Christianity teaches that we should love God and neighbor, but I don't see a great deal of that love in the so-called Christian society that surrounds us. In the Native American Church, sitting inside the tepee, our tabernacle, we are inside our Mother's womb where defenses and power plays aren't needed. We can be as God made us, which ultimately is why we feel moved to praise him. Laying defenses aside, we can bare our souls to one another, confessing our mistakes and asking for God's, and our neighbor's, forgiveness. In our way of speaking, we can say *ah-ho* to one another. This is what life is all about: becoming again the way that God created us and intends us to be.

This is the way I was raised in the Native American Church. And — if I may come back to myself and the name that my great-grandfather conferred on me, *Kikawunga*, "To Rise Up" — I try to live up to that name. I try to be a part of the bridge that spans what our Grandfathers understood about creation and the way the world is today with its uncertainty as to what life is about. Five hundred years ago the people on this continent had the same worldview. They saw themselves set within (and an integral part of) something great and wonderful that drew them compellingly to live in accord with its beauty and harmony. This was true all the way from the Bering Strait to Tierra del Fuego. Then other people arrived, bringing with them strange ideas. Turmoil and confusion have been their legacy.

What we in the Native American Church can do to reverse that legacy is to keep our ceremonial life intact down to its exact details. Cutting and preparing the firewood, erecting the tepee, building the altar, tying the water drum — everything must be done with utmost precision, exactly as our ancestors prescribed. For it is attention to details that preserves the sanctity of our traditions, and if they lose their holiness there is no point in continuing them.

I had a wonderful experience a number of years ago. A friend invited me to come to his new home and pray with him that God would bless it and the family it sheltered. He wanted it to be a sanctuary, a haven for those he loved. Glad to comply, I traveled from Nebraska to New Mexico to perform this errand for my friend. When I arrived and was preparing for the ceremony, my friend introduced me to an astrophysicist, a white who was visiting him. I had the opportunity to talk with this eminent gentleman scientist who, I learned, had had a part in discovering black holes in the Milky Way.

In the evening I told my host that I was going to give him the tepee I had brought with me and that he should watch carefully how things were done so he could repeat them thereafter in precisely the traditional way. Before sunrise the next morning I went outdoors and, facing in the direction from which the sun would rise, I prayed on the spot where the tepee was to be raised. When the sun came over the horizon, I marked the spot.

After breakfast, as we raised the tepee, built the altar, and prepared the firewood, I noticed that the astrophysicist was watching us as intently as was my host. It turned out that it was his fiftieth birthday, so when darkness fell and the house-blessing ceremony began we included him in our prayers, wishing him continued health and a long and happy life. He really enjoyed our Church's birthday songs for him, but the striking point is what happened toward daybreak as our ceremony was concluding. As we were singing our fourth and final morning song, the sun came over the horizon and hit the main pole of the tepee dead center.

"That astonished me," the astrophysicist told us later, at breakfast. "I had no idea you Indians were such technicians. Astronomy is my profession, and I can assure you that the direction your ancestors gave you for orienting the tepee so the first rays of the sun would be aligned to the tepee's doorway and its main pole were less than a hundredth of a degree off." He intended that as a compliment, of course, but I found myself saying, "Would you believe right on?" He thought for a moment and replied, "That could be. Yes. Right on."

Those last two words of his sum up my feelings about the teachings of the Native American Church. If you are faithful to them, you discover that they are right on.

An important word in the Winnebago language is *woshkun*. It means "Way, a way to be," and it sums up a great deal of our way of life. Central to that way, as I have said, is our sacred Medicine, Peyote; or as we call it in our language, *ma-ca-wa-ca-chugra*, so let me return to that. In Isaiah 29:4 it is written: "Then deep from the earth you shall speak, from low in the dust your words shall come; your voice shall come from the ground like the voice of a ghost, and your speech shall whisper out of the dust." We Indians hear that verse as referring to our sacred Peyote plant. Jesus was born in a part of the world that was semiarid. Water was a precious commodity. Life was difficult, especially for the Jews who had to live under Roman oppression. It was equally difficult for the Christians, once they became a distinct sect. They too were persecuted, reviled, tortured, and killed.

My grandfather taught us that it is the same with us today. Many of our tribes live on arid land where there isn't much water. Our holy Medicine comes from such land, and bears witness to the passage in the Bible I just quoted, for the Peyote plant comes to us as the voice of God arising from the earth. If Jesus was God incarnate in human form, our holy Peyote is God incarnate in plant form. And, like Jesus, it teaches us to love our fellowmen. The parallels continue, for Indians live in turmoil today, oppressed as were the Jews and early Christians. The saying, "The only good Indian is a dead Indian," is a grim reminder of that fact.

A final parallel between our Church and the early Christians carries a note of hope. Jesus ascended from the grave and promised to return to the earth triumphant. My grandfather linked this with Isaiah's thought that truth will rise from the ground. Those ideas apply not only to Peyote, but to our Church as well. It too will prevail.

That is what my maternal grandfather left for us to think about, but I want to say something about my paternal grandfather as well. His mother belonged to the Thunder Clan of our Winnebago tribe. He grew up in our traditional ways, then went away to school, graduating from Carlisle Institute. When he returned home, Christian missionaries used him as an interpreter, so he learned their religion, but he continued to be impressed with his indigenous Church. Eventually he joined it, but he soon realized that the life he was living didn't accord with the directives he was receiving from its fire. So as he ingested the Medicine he started to pray that the Creator would help him overcome some of his human faults.

During one of those prayers he saw a flame of light detach itself from the fireplace and exit the tepee through its door. Instinctively he got up and followed it. It led him eastward to a cliff. As he was standing by it, wondering why the light had led him there, he noticed that there were steps up the face of the cliff. He mounted them. When he reached the top he found himself standing on a broad, flat tableland. Walking across it, he was still wondering why God had brought him there when suddenly he looked down and saw written on the ground in front of him the story of Jesus' baptism. Looking around, he saw himself standing on an enormous open Bible and realized that this was God's answer to his prayer for a different life.

A few moments later the light that had guided him up the cliff reversed its course. It led him back to the tepee where it rejoined the sacred fire. At that moment my grandfather felt his spirit reenter his body which (he then realized) had not left its place in the sacred circle. During a break in the singing he told the Roadman, the leader of the meeting, that he wanted to be baptized, and because of his vision the baptism should be in Jesus' name. This came as a total surprise to the assembly, but the Roadman complied with the request. He told the Fireman (who had been tending the fire throughout the night) to bring water. When it arrived he directed the entire circle to stand up and, dipping an eagle feather into the water, he baptized my grandfather in the name of the Father, the Son, and the Holy Ghost.

That was the way the sacrament of baptism entered the ritual of my branch of the Native American Church. I relate this story to indicate its hospitality to other religious traditions. My grandfather's years as an interpreter for Christian missionaries had left their mark. When he realized that his way was to be in the Church of his people, he carried that influence with him, and in due course the institution of baptism took its place alongside our indigenous rituals.

Coming back to those indigenous ways, when we Indians want something that is important, we have a way of humbly asking for it. We look for a place that feels right to us, then clear that small part of our Grandmother Earth. We pick up the twigs, brush away the dry leaves, and smooth the ground to make it level. Then we draw on the ground a picture — either representational or symbolic — of what it is that we are imploring our Creator to give us. Our most recurrent request is for everlasting life, for no one really wants to die. But whatever the request, our elders assure us that if we inscribe it on Grandmother Earth's body and pray for it sincerely, we can then erase our markings and go on our way with assurance. If what we have asked for is worthy and in keeping with the order of things, it will be given to us. People who are unfamiliar with this custom call it magic and even sorcery, but this totally misses the mark. It is simply one of the ways we put our faith into practice, through a symbolic rite.

I hope that what I have written in this Introduction serves the book's purpose. To repeat what I said at the start, I feel that the best way to introduce my Church to a public who knows little about it is to say what it has meant to me, one of its humble but dedicated Roadmen.

But I want to end with our sacred Peyote, which is the pillar of our Church. I have ingested it since infancy. That I have never done so for kicks goes without saying. In every case I have approached it as a sacrament, and invariably it has lived up to that designation. Never has it caused me, or any Church member I have ever heard of, to hallucinate, and its directives have always been to live cleanly and with a loving, compassionate heart.

That such inspiration could come from a humble plant may not make rational sense to outsiders, but we insiders don't say "from," we say "through," for the powers and virtues of the plant are derived ultimately from the Great Spirit. The sense that Peyote makes to us is not rational but spiritual, proven by generations who have experienced its deliverances and tried their best to live up to them.

Please listen, dear readers, for we know whereof we speak. *Ah-ho!*

"Mother's Prayer," watercolor, by Archie Blackowl. Courtesy of Oklahoma
Indian Arts Gallery.

1

Voices of the
Native American Church

Continuing in the vein of the Introduction, this chapter presents firsthand accounts of what the Native American Church means to its members.

Testimonials that have been culled from existing literature are referenced. The other, usually longer, accounts were collected for this book and the film The Peyote Road *that is mentioned in the Preface. The statements have been adapted slightly to accommodate the difference between the spoken and the written word. Father Paul B. Steinmetz, S.J., author of* Pipe, Bible, and Peyote *(Knoxville: University of Tennessee Press, 1990), who lived among the Oglala Lakota Indians for twenty years, has helped considerably in compiling this chapter. — Editor*

Women and the Feminine

A long time ago one of my aunts, Ethel Blackbird, told me that Peyote can be used for many kinds of healings and that as women we should take it when we have our babies.

When it came time for me to do the woman's ritual of having my first child, my mother came from Washington state where she had been living. My labor pains started around four in the morning and she immediately got up and gave me some Medicine. This pulled my resources back inside of me and kept me calm. I didn't get scared. I realized that birthing is very

31

much a woman's act. Being calm enabled me to experience the birthing process clearly and calmly, consciously sensing and feeling what was going on.

This wasn't the case with the other eighteen women who were in the ward, at least not all of them. Some were screaming and crying, causing me to think, too, at the start, "This is going to get bad." But my mother said, "Just let the time flow along with what you're doing. The Medicine is taking care of you." I said, "Maybe you should give some Medicine to those other women."

Taking the Medicine also deepened the bonding process with my child. My mother told me that when my child came out it would wear the face of the Peyote, and in a way that happened, for around three in the afternoon when my son came into the world he had a yellow covering on his face that they had to peel off of him. We let him feel the elements at once, introducing him to the cold, the wind, and the ground.

My Grandma Louisa tells me that in earlier times women didn't participate in Peyote meetings. Part of the reason is that, as life-givers, women have powerful Medicine in themselves. We are powerful people. So it was only at dawn, when the Water Woman entered the tepee with her bucket of life-giving water, that other women would enter. The power of their prayers extended the prayers the men had said during the night, so that what they had asked for would be granted.

Loretta Afraid-of-Bear Cook, Lakota

I was still a little girl when there was a birthday meeting for my father. He told me, "I'm going to let you come into this meeting and sit with the grown-ups. This meeting is especially for you. Everyone is going to pray for you, and ask blessings for you and for your future, that someday you will be useful to your people."

So I agreed to go in. I sat by my grandfather, and he had little Peyote buttons that he had fixed and cleaned. He said, "Granddaughter, I want you to eat this Medicine because it's going to give you a good mind and make you have good health in your life." I started to eat it and thought to myself, "It's very bitter."

My father had instructed me to pray for everyone in the tepee, especially the chief, the drummer, the cedarman, and the fireman, so I started with the person by the door and went around the circle praying for everyone including those who were sick, for I had been told that the Peyote touches every soul that lives and gives it the special care and health it needs.

In the morning hours my father told me, "Even though you are underage, you are going to be the Water Woman and carry in the water for this meeting. To fill this role properly, you must understand that water is sacred. You females bring life into this world. You renew life. This is the meaning we all have in mind when the Water Woman brings in the water at the hour of daybreak. Because you are young and your future is coming to you, I want you to understand these things by performing this ritual."

He then took me outside and showed me how to carry the water into the tepee. I was to look to the east, and when I heard the morning songs and whistles I was to pray to the east for my health. Then I would carry the water into the tepee and pray over it before the pail was passed around the circle for people to drink.

The next time I was Water Woman was when I was sixteen. This time my father said, "Now you are becoming a young woman, so this will be the last Peyote meeting I will have for you. It's very important that when you carry the water into the tepee you remember everything I have taught you about its purpose in the meeting. Keep in mind all the people who have prayed for you in these meetings and kept you strong mentally and physically. Their prayers, blessed by the Medicine, will carry you through life. Never forget that when the women carry water into our meetings, this blesses not only the lives of those in the tepee, but all life and all creation."

I believed these things that my father told me then, and I believe them now, which is why I have remained in the Native American Church and will continue in it for the rest of my days. Recently my brother had a birthday meeting for his daughter. Now that our father is deceased it's up to us to continue our ways.

Patricia Mousetrail Russell, Southern Cheyenne

Children and Family

Four or five years ago I became aware of a sacred word. It's a word that we often say without thinking much about it.

I had asked my aunt about disciplining children at social gatherings, and she said, "I'm going to teach you a very sacred word." I said, "OK." So I'm sitting there and she looks at me and says, "Shhhhh," pressing a finger to her lips.

I sat quietly, waiting for her to tell me the sacred word, but all she did was quietly go about doing what she was doing. Finally after about twenty minutes I said, "Well, what are you going to do?" She said, "I'm teaching you the sacred word." I said, "I don't understand." She said, "Well, I said 'shhhh,' and you sat down and did what I told you to do, which shows that you are learning that sacred word." I said, "Well?"

She said, "'Shhhh' is the word that you should teach your children. Think back to social gatherings. Have you ever said that word to your children? I have, many times. It was a word that my mother often said to us. The word was used in our tepees. When our mother would say that word and give us a scathing look, we knew better than to move around. If things got critical, all she had to do was look at us and say, 'Shhhh.'"

We learned discipline in the tepee in the way that my aunt described. Once at a meeting my small son was walking by the soup bowls. It was a hot area and I didn't want him to be burned, so I swatted him on the butt.

After the meeting my uncles came up to me and said, "We didn't bring you up that way," and I became ashamed that I had hit my son. It helped me see that you teach your children by talking to them, not by hitting them. You teach them the sacred words and they will abide by them.

When I was very small they let me sleep through the all-night meetings, but there comes an age when children sit up with the adults. We call that the age of understanding. It comes to girls around seven or eight, and to boys about nine or ten.

My uncles say that if you want to learn something you take lots and lots of Medicine; you take it and you think about what you want to learn. So that's what we tell our children.

You tell them, "You take this Medicine. Tell it to pity you and let you understand what it is that you need to know. You listen to the prayers that are said tonight. Keep your minds on what they are praying for. When morning comes, pray for yourself and your family, but do that last. First think about the other things that go on during the night — the people that are offering tobacco and asking for help. That's the main purpose for your being here."

A month after my son was born we took him back to the reservation and my uncles took him to a ceremony. They tied feathers on his head, sang the naming song for him, and let Peyote look at him so it would be clear how he was being cared for.

Every year thereafter we have had a ceremony for him. During it my uncles — they tease me a lot, but they teach me a lot too — instruct me about raising my son, right down to advising breastfeeding, feeding the child from my own body. A great deal of the knowledge of traditional ways is incorporated in these Native American Church ceremonies. While my uncles advise me, my aunts tell my husband how he's supposed to be a father. Every year we are reminded of these things when it's time to have the ceremony for our son.

We talk about *ap-pa-paish*, being kind to things, and taking our Medicine helps us to take responsibility for ourselves and our children. We must be sure that we provide good homes for them, that we remain sober, and that we are generous with our people. We believe that children are like cameras; they photograph in their minds what they see us as parents doing. So it behooves us as parents to see to it that we are providing good environments for our children. The best thing we can do is to provide positive models for them.

Peyote has helped us in that, for it's been the heart of our family around which everything revolves. Every day we do something that involves the Medicine. I carry it in my purse and in my car. When I get in a bind I put Peyote on top of the dashboard so that it can see the road. When we go on trips we pray for good road conditions and that Peyote will guide us. In many ways like these, Peyote is at the heart of our family life. This gives us the opportunity to grow close to our children, to become best friends with them. When the time comes, they naturally move on to have friends of their own. But hopefully the guidance they've received at home and in our Church will carry them through.

Physically, the Medicine is hard to take; it has a harsh taste. To take it you have to talk to it, asking it to be good to you and to pity you. Then you thank it for the knowledge that it provides, and you keep it with you all the time. If we don't have Peyote in our home it feels scary. It feels unsafe.

My Grandpa Ben laid down prayers for specific meetings — *lam-buttes* — in which we pray that the heartbeat of our ceremonial drum will carry on forever in our community. We pray that as our children grow up they will focus on that heartbeat and keep it close to them. In doing this we tie together a lot of different families and different age groups.

Loretta Afraid-of-Bear Cook

The Medicine

We can't explain our religion. To understand it you have to eat its Medicine.   *Anonymous*[1]

Our favorite term for Peyote is "Medicine," and to us it is a portion of the body of Christ, even as the communion bread is believed to be a portion of Christ's body by Christian churches. In the Bible, Christ spoke of a comforter who was to come. Sent by God, this comforter came to the Indians in the form of this holy Medicine. We know whereof we speak. We have tasted of God and our eyes have been opened.

It is utter folly for scientists to attempt to analyze this Medicine. Can science analyze God's body? No! No white man can understand it. It came from God. It is a part of God's body. God's Holy Spirit envelops it. It was given exclusively to Indians and God never intended that white men should understand it. It cures us of our temporal ills, as well as ills of a spiritual nature. It takes away the desire for strong drink. I myself have been cured of a loathsome disease, too horrible to mention. So have hundreds of others. Hundreds of confirmed drunkards have been dragged from their downward way.

Albert Hensley, Winnebago[2]

Vegetation and trees, the rivers, sunshine, the moon in the night sky, thunder and lightning, birds flying in the air — it seems like God made this world and left it just the way he made it. And we found this Medicine.

I'll be ninety-four on my next birthday, so if there's an example of someone who's been using Peyote all his life, I guess I'm he. I feel that I would die for this Medicine, it has meant so much to my life. My people use it and find spiritual guidance in it. I'm poor in spirit, but when I sit in the meeting and partake of the Medicine I concentrate and think and meditate while the meeting is going on. I think of how I want to be blessed and who I want to pray for. The outside world disappears in my mind while I'm in the tepee. I feel humble, and the good thoughts that I think there help me.

Truman Dailey, Otoe-Missouri

I have never seen colors or experienced delusions of any sort while taking Peyote. What it feels like is that I am sitting right by God the Creator. I communicate with him. Of course he isn't there physically, but spiritually I sense that he is near me. And whatever I pray for — good health, or other good things in life — I feel that he listens; he hears me. Other than that special sense of closeness, the experience isn't remarkable.

The Medicine is bitter, and I wouldn't want to take it for any reason other than a religious one, or for reasons of health. Once in a meeting I did see little whirlwinds flying around the tepee, but I credit that to the power of the fire. I wasn't frightened, or think that I was seeing spooky things.

Part of the experience of being close to God is that the Medicine gets bad stuff out of you. If you have evil thoughts or are in a poor frame of mind generally, you are going to see all that clearly. In this way, if you're not living your life well, Peyote purifies you. It helps to clean your spirit. I have never seen anyone in our Church act crazily, but I have heard many testimonials of gratitude to the Creator and prayers for forgiveness.

Patricia Mousetrail Russell, Southern Cheyenne

Peyote goes all over my body. I feel it; it's working. My mind is clear. Before I didn't think much about what's right, but with Peyote I know it's God working, the God who gave it to us. I feel good because God is going to take care of me. I have nothing to worry about, nothing to be afraid of because the Almighty is at work.   *Dewey Neconish, Menomini*[3]

Peyote is not like a narcotic. When you eat it, your mind turns to the Great Spirit. In one song I can learn what might take twenty or twenty-five years in school.

Bernard Ice, blind Oglala Lakota[4]

The purpose of Peyote is to clear the mind. The mind functions in all kinds of manners, thinking of many things. When you take the Medicine, God's spirit power is in the Medicine. It clears the mind. You can see clearly and you can talk to God. We don't have much education and we don't use big words, so we use the Medicine. If you take Peyote in a meeting and think about things, insight will come to you.

Francis Mesteth, Oglala Lakota[5]

Peyote is power. A tremendous power pervades the tepee during a meeting. It will take all your lifetime to know only a small part of the power that is there.

Similar statements by a Navajo and a Crow, combined[6]

When you take Peyote, you have an inner eye that clears things up and tells you what is right and wrong. My father, Charles, told me that if you take a lot of Peyote your eye clears and you can see what is important.

Joe American Horse, Oglala Lakota[7]

In the first creation God himself used to talk to people and tell them what to do. Long after, Christ came among the white people and told them what to do. Then God gave us Indians Peyote. That's how we found God. *A Kiowa*[8]

The Medicine is the main thing of all. It's our life. Nothing else can do much without the herb the Creator gave us.

A Washoe[9]

Missionaries say we use a drug and that it makes us crazy. It isn't so. I've used Peyote a long time, and I know better. Used in the right way, it's good for us Indians. It wasn't given to the white man; it was given to the Indian so he can get some enlightenment from God through it. *A Chippewa*[10]

Our holy Medicine has within it four powers: love, hope, charity, and faith. That's what this Medicine is about. It helps us to interpret life. It helps our minds to open and become tolerant, even of our weaknesses. We acknowledge our weaknesses, and pray to overcome them.

Ted Strong, Yakima Nation, Washington

I didn't think I could pray in public, in the presence of others. Then one night in a meeting I heard this man praying and I became curious and followed closely what he said. It sounded all right to me. I could understand his Chippewa words and tongue. And then I realized that the man I was listening to was myself. That surprised me. Sometimes unusual things happen in meetings.   *A Chippewa*[11]

The Medicine lets us see the personal significance of what goes on inside and outside us. It causes us to ask, "What do these things mean for me?" As for the answers Peyote gives us, we know absolutely that they are not our inventions. They come from God.   *Anonymous*[12]

There's no preaching in our ceremony. We get our knowledge directly from the Almighty. We don't need anyone telling us what the word is. That's what Peyote is for. You take that, and the Medicine will do the rest. God will talk to you himself. You don't need a Bible.   *Anonymous*[13]

When we eat our Medicine we first become pitiful. We grow nauseated and dizzy. Some experience choking, shortness of breath, cramps, and tremors. Some become anxious and depressed; they feel abandoned and think they are going to die. But then the spirit in Peyote tells us: "I have caused you to go through all this suffering, for had I not done so, you would never have heard of the proper religion."   *Anonymous*[14]

During the meeting Jesus spoke to me. I asked him, "What is this Peyote?" And Jesus Christ said to me, "Those who hated me crucified me on the cross. And then after my blood dropped to the earth from my heart, there grew up from the earth vegetation, and that was Peyote, and Peyote is my blood."
A Navajo[15]

Symbolism

Everything represents.   *A Menomini*[16]

The Native American Church is a poor, humble Church. We sit on the ground or on our knees all night long. We meditate, concentrate, and pray to the Creator all night long for blessings for our children.

We don't have fancy churches or TV evangelists. We keep things simple, the way they were given to us. Our ceremonial objects are four: our staff, our drum, our gourd, and our whistle that's made of eagle bones.

We were told that our drum represents the heartbeat. When we're inside our mother's womb, floating in fluids and in darkness, the first thing that we hear is our mother's heartbeat. *Ka-tun, ka-tun.*

To the unborn child, this heartbeat represents everything in life that's good. My Sioux relatives call it the Good Red Road, my Din-eh people, the Navajo, call it the *Ho-jo-ne* way. Peace, harmony, serenity, tranquility, contentment, love and affection. When we're with our mothers everything is all right, and her heartbeat is all that we hear for our first nine months.

All our drums, but especially our ceremonial water drum, represent the heartbeat that we initially heard.

In addition, though, the drum represents the heartbeat of Mother Earth where everything is in peace and harmony and unity, the way that God made things. Some of the power of the Thunder Beings is in this ceremonial drum of ours.

My wife and I have a daughter, seventeen months old. Whenever our daughter cries, or needs to be changed, or has her feelings hurt, my wife picks her up and everything becomes all right because she hears her mother's heartbeat. She feels warmth, and peace, and tranquility. She knows that she belongs. She knows that she's special and belongs somewhere.

Johnny White Cloud, Otoe-Missouri/Creek/Seminole

I don't think that those who are not Native Americans can understand our Holy Sacrament. We Indians are close to fire and the fireplaces that protect the Medicine and its effect on our minds.

The Medicine brings us closer to the fireplace, and at the same time closer to God the Spirit, who gives us good lives and good outlooks on the future.

Robert Billie White Horse, Past President of the Native American Church of Navajoland

All of the important things that life requires are woven into the ceremony. The entire ceremony is symbolic of our dependence on and use of things in our environment: fire, water, plants, and animals. *Old Crow*[17]

Worship

We don't need cathedrals or million dollar churches. Wherever we are — in the mountains, by a stream, anywhere — we can stop, sit down, pray to our Creator, and that's our church.

John Emhoola, Kiowa Tribe, Oklahoma

We use fire in our ceremonies because we can't get along without it. It keeps us warm and cooks our food. We put cedar on the fireplace and make our offerings to the Almighty in prayer through that fire. *Bernard Ice*[18]

The star on the bottom of our drum is the Morning Star. One of our Morning Star songs says, "One day He will come from the east and He wants me to prepare to meet Him." In this song we ask for life everlasting and peace. As you beat the drum, the sound goes south to the land of the spirits and to those who are there. Some are drummers, some roadmen, firemen, cedar men, people who were in meetings with us, our singers. The echo of this drum brings the spirits back so that from the outside they can partake of the meeting and listen to the way we remember them in our prayers. Then they bless us in return. *Lawrence Hunter, Minneconjou Lakota*[19]

Sometimes I am sitting here at home all alone, but I am not alone. I have a drum, water, and a gourd. I sing the songs of my church and my worries are all gone. I feel good again, and refreshed. The drum has seven stones in it, which stand for the seven Indian sacraments of life — the Holy Peyote, the dirt Half Moon, the fire, water, corn, meat, and fruit. On the bottom of the drum the rope forms a star. When the drum is pounded it's like the speaking in tongues the Bible reports. The skin on the drum is animal hide that is used for clothing.

Bernard Ice, blind Oglala Lakota[20]

When you beat the drum, it brings out the sounds that represent the Thunders. The sounds will go a long way through the valleys and canyons. So by pounding the drum the sound goes up to the Almighty. Since it goes along the horizons, it must go up too. Because the Thunders are the source of rain, we put water in the drum. *Bernard Red Cloud*[21]

During a meeting the roadman's staff, which is the staff of life, goes to everyone who is present. Each time a man or woman gets hold of the staff, he puts prayers on it and then gives it to the next person. So the staff goes around and collects good thoughts and prayers and lays all of them at the altar, which is the sacred fire. You don't go between the staff and the altar because the prayers are going up from the staff through the fire. I have the feeling that little strings run from the staff to the fire. If you go between the staff and the fire, you break the strings from the man who is singing.

We use sage too. Today you can wash your hands, but in the old days we used sage. When you take the staff and the Peace Pipe, you hold them with hands that have been rubbed with sage. Your hands have been purified so that they are worthy to grasp the staff and the Peace Pipe.

Bernard Red Cloud[22]

We talk to the Medicine in the same way that we talk to trees and rivers.

Paris Williams, Ponca

We burn incense for purification, and we eat Peyote to come into communion with the Great Spirit. But we also have to have something to offer to the Great Spirit. He accepts our offerings through the ascending smoke of our sacred tobacco. That's why it's special for us.

We try to keep the drum going during our sermons. We try not to talk too long, or pray too long. Just keep that heartbeat drum going. Then, through our Medicine, we have this spiritual experience.

Johnny White Cloud

During the meeting the singing sounded lovely, the Indian dresses looked very beautiful, and in the morning the sun rose on the best world I ever saw. I felt young and good in every way.

A Chiricahua Apache[23]

About that time in the meeting the old roadman told the story of our origins. It seemed like I lived right through it. To understand it I had to live through it.

Anonymous[24]

We make our own tepee, and we sit right on the ground and worship the Almighty. Because we're Indians we sit on the ground. The Almighty gave us this Mother Earth, and we sit there and pray to Him and ask Him for what we want.

A Menomini woman in her fifties[25]

Religious Sentiments: Reverence, Humility, Awe, and Love

There are certain times in a meeting when you can feel a presence. A feeling comes in the meeting — it's a holy feeling, the presence of the Spirit of God that's in the midst of these people. You feel that presence. It makes you want to pray deep in your heart.

A Menomini man in his forties[26]

Last week we admitted a newspaper woman who wanted to find out about the Native American Church. When she came out of the tepee in the morning she told us how humble she felt. That's true of us too. Our Holy Sacrament, Peyote, teaches us humility.

Paris Williams, Ponca

Throughout all the years that I had lived on earth, I now realized that I had never known anything holy. Now, for the first time, I knew something holy.

John Rave, Winnebago, after his first Peyote meeting[27]

I'm glad I joined the Native American Church and used the Medicine, since it really made me think about the Almighty and how far away I had gotten from Him.

Beatrice Weasel Bear[28]

The Peyote to me is my Bible. I know what I should be doing and shouldn't be doing. When I take that Peyote, I feel humble and respectful all the time.   *Larry Etsitty, Navajoland*[29]

This Medicine's got hope in it. It's got faith in it. It's got love in it. And it's got charity in it. So fill up all the fireplaces. Fill them up with those four words.

Willie Riggs, Sr., Navajo Roadman

Moral Impact

This Peyote has done me a world of good. It put me on the right road. It has caused me to put aside all intoxicating liquor; I now have no desire for whiskey, beer, or any strong drinks. I have no desire for tobacco. If I keep on using this Peyote, I'm going to be an upright man towards God.   *A Menomini*[30]

When I started eating that Medicine it told me something. I found out I was a sinner. Then I commenced to think why I was like that. I ate some more, and I found out that Peyote teaches me what is right. From then on I've tried to behave myself.   *A Menomini*[31]

Chief Peyote tells us that our meetings are to make Indians good, to make them friends, and to make them stop fighting. When we eat Peyote we feel towards others a warm glow in our hearts as if they were our brothers.

Ralph Kochampanaskin[32]

This is all that I know. When I started eating this Medicine I began to see everything. I no longer quarreled with anyone. I no longer was angry with anyone. That's it. When I started to eat this Medicine I began to think of the Great Spirit always, every day.   *A Menomini woman in her seventies*[33]

Tradition

Our music, our songs, the ceremonial objects that we use in our tepees — these are all good for us Indian peoples. I'm going to stand up for that. I'm going to stand up for our Indian ways — that's number one. I'm going to continue to teach my children and grandchildren our Indian culture and try to be a role model for them. Our religion is too beautiful, too refined, too rich to abandon. This is where I can communicate with my Creator.

I did once leave my Church. I went to the Methodist Church and the Catholic Church, but they couldn't fill my heart. I missed my Indian music, my Indian songs. I couldn't hear Indian languages spoken in those churches.

My ancestors who have gone on have left us their ways for us to carry on, and I intend to follow them because I know that's what they would want us to do. Five hundred years of oppression lie behind us, and now again our religion is at stake. They've taken our land, they've taken our water. Now our religion is all we have left.

I hope that five hundred years from now our tradition will still be intact. For our children, our grandchildren, and those yet unborn.   *John Emhoola*

Once you come into the tepee and sit down and use this Medicine, our holy Medicine, you belong, no matter what tribe you are. You always did belong, but now you realize it. You belong to this Circle, because you are one of God's red race of children.

We feel the way we felt when our mothers wrapped their arms around us when we were children. And before that, the way we felt when we were in our mothers' wombs.

Johnny White Cloud

I wasn't born into the Native American Church. I was introduced to it fourteen years ago when I was fifty-eight.

I was born on the Klamath reservation and by the age of eight was taken from my home and put into a parochial school. The remainder of my education was in boarding schools. These were difficult times for me. I was separated from my family and stripped of my language, my culture, and my identity. Eventually I became an alcoholic.

At the age of thirty-six I stopped drinking and began a life of recovery through Alcoholics Anonymous. Fifteen years later I was introduced to my first sweatlodge ceremony. That was the beginning of my introduction to the way my ancestors had lived, and to this day I receive spiritual guidance through Native American ceremonies.

In parochial schools I was exposed to Christianity but it didn't meet my spiritual needs. It was Native spirituality that brought my life into a totally new perspective. I learned how to live and how to understand the Creator in a natural way.

Alfred Leo Smith, Klamath Nation

My experience with Peyote, the holy sacrament of our Church, began with my mother and her serious illness. Our family tried the standard ways to heal her, but when they all failed we sought out the Native American Church, hoping that its sacred Medicine would work where other medicines had failed. We took to the Church from the very beginning, not knowing what we were getting into.

What happened was that my mother lived for two years beyond the three months that her physicians predicted when they diagnosed her disease. Our mother spent much of those two years explaining and clarifying the values that she and our father had raised us children by. This was of immense value to us and we owe the gift to the Medicine. If her life had not been extended, she would not have been able to transmit her values to us securely, teaching us their meaning and explaining why we should remain true to them.

Floyd Flores, Native American Church of Southern Arizona

Petition, Protection, and Guidance

Well, Great Spirit, the time has now come; I am going to pray to you where I'm standing. Please let everything be abundant, so that we may exist well on this earth where we live. We thank you, Great Spirit above for allowing us to live up to the present. We pray you to give strength to every one of us. Hold the hands of each one of my children. Give them strength. Give them that which is good in the future, and make them stand erect here on earth where we live.

An anonymous Menomini[34]

Great Spirit who is all, I am going to give you thanks now. And now I am telling you in advance that we have all come here to this house, which you gave us, to pray to be purified. Now we are going to enter to pray to you all night. These, my brothers and sisters, will pray to you. Please keep carefully in mind whatever they will ask of you. Also, my relatives have come to visit us. They are going to pray to you for whatever is in their thought. So in advance we are telling you, here, that we are going to enter this house which you have given us to pray to you.   *Thomas Wayka, Menomini*[35]

They prayed for me when Vietnam was going on. I took the Medicine with me. I was a paratrooper and scuba diver in the First Force Rican Platoon at the tail end of Vietnam. The Medicine took me over there and it brought me back.

I prayed with the smoke [sacred tobacco]: "Creator God,

"Osage Peyote Man," pochois print, by Stephen Mopope. Courtesy Oklahoma Indian Arts Gallery.

take me over there and bring me back with nothing wrong with me. Give me an honorable discharge that will make my people proud of me. I won't forget this prayer when I come back."

Today I am going on that same prayer.

Johnny White Cloud

We were living a good life, but we had a bad experience in the death of Deloris, our teen-age daughter. Different people talked to us. "You belong to the Native American Church," they said. "Now the Almighty wants to know if you mean business. He took one of your children to see if you are going to continue to believe in him or not. Are you going to think of her in heaven or lose faith and turn to a bad life?"

I was tempted to think that as I had always lived a good life, there may be no God. Earlier there had been music and joy in the Native American Church, but when Deloris died I didn't enjoy the music at the funeral meeting. There was nothing there. Oh, it was there, but my mind said that it wasn't. It took a year for it to come back.

Now it's up to me and my family. If we want to see Deloris, we have to keep on the right path. That's what the Peyote has done for me. It showed me that and has gotten me this far.

Bernard Red Cloud[36]

We find out things from Peyote at night, just like seeing things in the daytime.   *Anonymous*[37]

Visions

I had a vision of being inside the drum that I was beating. Every time I beat it, it looked like the water was coming up. I wanted to get out but I couldn't. If I beat the drum slowly, the water would go down, but I couldn't get away from it.

The last song I remember singing was the Chief Song. As I sang it, I kept muttering to myself, "Great Spirit, have pity on me." As I looked at the Chief Peyote, he was just a little old man — wrinkled up, stringy grey hair, barefooted, sitting on the mound. I couldn't get past him. He was sitting there like Father Time, watching me. And I couldn't hide anything that came to my mind because he knew it all. Then I began singing again and I came out of it.

The only thing Peyote told me was, "Try to do it right." He said that if I didn't I was going to hurt myself and somebody else, too. *Lawrence Hunter*[38]

In my very first meeting I saw a vision in the fireplace, a vision I will never forget. There was the Half Moon altar, then a space, the fire, the waterbird ashes, and the tail further on down. The Half Moon and the Peyote were sitting on top, way up there. It looked real nice up there. The Peyote was on top like a crown. In between I saw a dark abyss. The body of the water bird was sparkling, like a shining city. When I looked at the city, I saw a lot of evil things going on there. Further on down, where the tail part was, I saw human skulls and bones covered with snakes.

It came to me that if a person stays on top, he will be all

right. But if he falls down into the abyss and the city, he will end up with the bones and snakes. If a person doesn't follow the Peyote road, he will end up with death, real death.

A middle-aged Lakota woman[39]

Healing

I am ninety-six years old now, and when people ask me how long I have been taking this Medicine I say since before I was born. I say that because my mother took some Peyote the night before she delivered me. First she offered a prayer, and then she swallowed the Medicine. I was born about noon the following day, and as soon as she could get up and around, the first thing she did was make some Medicine tea and give me some of it. To understand all this you need to know that I wasn't her first child. There had been two boys before me, but neither of them survived. My mother wanted to be sure that I would make it, and that's why she took the Medicine at the time of my delivery and gave me some as soon as she was able.

To help you understand her great faith in our Medicine I have to go back four or five years. About three years before she gave birth to me she got so she couldn't walk, and to explain what happened then I need to go back still farther and tell you about her upbringing.

Her mother — my grandmother — was an orphan who was brought up in a Christian Bible School and was separated from our people, so she grew up Christian and raised my mother that way. But when she was of marriageable age she went to visit the nearby Ote tribe. One of the boys there liked her and they got married. The family she married into was 100 percent

Indian, but her upbringing had been Christian. Then a strange
malady beset her. The doctors never did understand what it
was, but she became crippled. She couldn't walk. With her
Christian upbringing she prayed as hard as she could to Jesus,
but it didn't help. She kept getting worse.

Then something happened that turned out to be important. Her family was on its way to a tribal meeting of some sort
and the house where they stopped to spend the night had a
tepee behind it — there was going to be a Peyote meeting that
night, but it began to pour and the ground in the tepee turned
to mud so they held the meeting in the house. That was the first
Peyote meeting my mother had ever attended. Around midnight a bucket of water was passed around and she drank some.
That water hadn't touched the ground because it had been collected in pans that people had put out to catch the rain. After
they drank the water they started to sing, and then they offered
her the Medicine. They told her that if she took the Medicine
and prayed with all the faith she could manage, it might help
her. She consumed it, prayed, and when the meeting was over
she began to get well. Within a month she was walking.

I don't know, of course, but it seems like her faith was equally strong when she was a Christian, but when she got on the Indian side of the religion and took the Medicine, it seems like
that's what made the difference and enabled her to walk again.

Truman Dailey, Otoe-Missouri

Two years ago I fell ill. It was scary for me because I seemed to
have a blood disorder. The doctors were talking about sending
me to Minnesota to have me treated for leukemia.

Four days before my birthday my parents put on a prayer service for me. They rolled the sacred tobacco, gave me Medicine, fanned me with the waterbird fan and prayed for me.

Four days later I went to the hospital. My blood count was normal, and I gained back the weight I lost.

I think, too, of the miracle that happened to my Grandpa Philip, from whom I get my middle name, Afraid-of-Bear. Once when he was home on leave from the service there was a prayer ceremony for a young man who was desperately ill. Grandpa was the Fireman at this meeting and Peyote was placed in the center of the room so everybody could eat as much at they wanted to. In ceremonies that were specifically for healing, people would ingest as much as they could and more, to increase the Medicine's power.

As the evening wore on, it seemed clear that the young man was crying. So when midnight arrived and it was time for Grandpa to pray officially as Fireman, he asked the Creator to take his goodness, his wholesomeness and strength, and give them to this younger, dying man. He said he would be willing to lay down his remaining years for the man who had not experienced as much of life as he had.

The young man survived his crisis and did pull through. But Grandpa — the next day, while chasing horses, keeled over with a heart attack. That was sad, but it happened the way he wanted it to. Peyote listened to him, and granted what he asked.   *Loretta Afraid-of-Bear Cook*

One time I got sick; my eye hurt. I kept going to doctors in three towns until my money ran out, but they couldn't help me. I grew more and more blind until finally I couldn't see at all.

One evening my stepmother made some Peyote tea and suggested I drink it. At my wit's end, I did; I drank a lot of it. Then, as it was near bedtime anyway, I went upstairs and laid down. Pretty soon I knew that the Peyote was working on me. It felt good. I laid there all night thinking, *I'm going blind.*

As dawn was breaking I heard a knocking. At first I thought it must be my heart, but then I concluded that it must be a bird. I sat up in bed, looked toward the window, and my gosh, I could see. I could see the bird and the whole outdoors. That Peyote cured me in a single night.

Dewey Neconish, Menomini[40]

We had a tepee meeting in Scottsbluff at Joe Sierra's place for a Navajo couple whose daughter was in the hospital with double pneumonia. Her father asked for our prayers. Towards the main smoke in the morning, the staff came to me and I said, "We are going to sing some songs and try to help out in every way we can. I have children of my own."

I started singing, but somehow the song was different. When I closed my eyes I seemed to be wandering around in hills somewhere. I was trying to find something. I had this long stick, and I was poking around for something, but I couldn't find it. So I cut the song off and started another one. I kept going from one song to another like that, but I still couldn't find what I was looking for. When I opened my eyes, I saw that I was making the people restless the way I was rambling through those songs. I knew the songs, but they seemed different to me now. As I was getting nowhere I went on to the last song.

It was high pitched, and during it I found the thing I was looking for. It was a root. I picked it up, and put a piece of it in my mouth and started chewing it; I also stuck a piece of it in my pocket. About that time the drumbeat came out right and the Roadman started blowing his whistle and started yelling, "Heya, heya." Everybody started flapping their feather fans, and I kept singing that song and I got through my turn in the circle.

The girl's mother came over and grasped me and said, "Thank you. As you sang the last song, my little girl came to the door in a vision and she was well."

After the meeting they went to the hospital to see their daughter, and when they came back they had the little girl with them. Finding the root in the vision had the power to heal her.   *Lawrence Hunter*[41]

Joe Sierra had tuberculosis real bad. The hospital said he was going to die. He went to Oklahoma, and our people doctored him and gave him a lot of Medicine. Pretty soon he had a vision. He was wandering in a desert. Somebody told him to pray to his grandfather. At first he thought of his natural grandfather, but the voice kept on repeating, "Remember your grandfather." Then he thought of his great-grandfathers, and other grandfathers in an Indian way, but he still heard that voice. Then all of a sudden it dawned on him that the voice was telling him to pray to the Great Spirit Grandfather. He did so, and he got well.   *Beatrice Weasel Bear*[42]

I have two brothers, both of whom suffered seriously from pneumonia while they were young. My uncle, *Yo-ma-ton*, was a Medicine man and, using his buffalo horn with the Medicine, he cured first Parker and then Farrell.   *John Emhoola*

When my wife was young she contracted tuberculosis which left her blind. Children teased and made fun of her, but one of my grandfathers in Wisconsin felt sorry for her and said, "Tonight we're going to have a meeting for *My-tu-zunt*, my granddaughter. Anyone who wants to can come pray for her."

They sat up all night. My grandfather took some tea Medicine that had aged for about a year, put some drops in my wife's eyes, and had her drink some. Then he sang what we call doctor songs that ask God to have pity on our children.

There and then, as he washed his granddaughter's eyes, the scales fell from them and she could see. Today she helps me make tepees, does beadwork, does ribbon work, and is an accomplished person.   *Johnny White Cloud*

I have a brother, Gerald Kozad — he's actually my cousin but I call him my brother — whose bones were so badly crushed in a car accident that an Oklahoma City doctor said he would never walk again. But he came on crutches, once, to a Peyote ceremony at my sister's place and towards its close he told my father, who was the Roadman, that he was going to walk out of the tepee. My father protested and wanted to help him, but he said, "No, it was revealed to me tonight that I will walk out of here."

He did, and to this day the doctors are unable to account for what happened.   *Andy Kozad, Kiowa*

My mother tells me that she is living proof of the power of this Medicine.

As a little girl she couldn't walk — they didn't know what was wrong with her, but she couldn't walk. She would sit by her tepee door, watching the kids running around and playing, and wish that she could be out with them. But she couldn't be.

Then one day she saw an old man walking by. She didn't know who he was; everybody just called him Grandpa. She didn't know that he was a Medicine man — this was back when Medicine men were still powerful — but she found herself saying to him, "Grandpa, come heal me. Doctor me so that I can go out and play with the other kids."

The old man went to the ground and blessed himself, and there were tears in his eyes. When he got up he called to the criers in the camp to call people to put up a tepee, that there was going to be a doctoring to heal this little girl who had asked for help.

The criers went through the camp, got the men to raise the tepee, and the healing ceremony was held. The first night my mother, lying in the tepee, saw the men tie the Medicine man's hands and feet and wrap him in a buffalo robe. Around midnight she looked at him and saw him begin to rise from the ground. He was still wrapped in the buffalo robe, but he wasn't touching the ground. She didn't know how he did this; all she said was that it must have been his Spirit.

Four nights in a row they had a Peyote ceremony. Everyone was taking the Medicine, and they also gave it to her.

On the morning of the fourth day the Medicine man opened the door of the tepee and said, "Granddaughter, you must get up and walk out of this tepee." My mother said she didn't think that she could, but she got up and walked out. That's why she says she's living proof of the power of this Medicine, and why she tells me always to respect it.

Patricia Mousetrail Russell, Southern Cheyenne

New Life and Behavior Change

I started using Peyote when I came back from the Army in 1962. I stopped using liquor because it was not right to use it with the Medicine. I told all these people when they came to my meeting, "You guys better straighten up. This liquor doesn't go with the Medicine." White people say liquor and gas don't go together. It's the same with Medicine. Liquor and Medicine don't go together either. *Irvin Tachonie, Navajo*

It's been twenty-three years that I've lived a life of sobriety. I don't smoke cigarettes like I used to. I don't drink alcohol or use any kind of drugs because of the life that I now live in the Native American Church. That's what it's done for me, for my family and my relatives on both sides: my Winnebago in-laws, my Sioux relatives, my Menomini relatives, my Creek and Seminole and Ottawa and Iowa, my people back home in Oklahoma.

This is what the Church has done for me, but we don't call the Native American Church a religion. We call it a way of life that we live every day, twenty-four hours every day, not just once a week.   *Johnny White Cloud*

I'm into my sixth year of recovery from alcoholism. I'm off the bottle now, but the temptation is still there. When I go to Peyote I pray God to forgive my old alcoholism and to keep me sober.

Over the years Peyote has taught me many things, though actually it was God who taught them to me through Peyote.

Andy Kozad

When I first used Peyote I became deathly sick. It seemed like I vomited several bottles of whiskey, several plugs of tobacco, and two bulldogs. This accumulation of filth represented all the sins I had ever committed. With its expulsion I became pure and clean in the sight of God, and I knew that by the continued use of Peyote I would remain in that condition. I was transformed — a new man.   *A Winnebago*[43]

When I first took Peyote my heart was filled with murderous thoughts. I wanted to kill my brother and sister. All my thoughts were fixed on the warpath. Some evil spirit possessed me. I even desired to kill myself.

Then I ate this Medicine and everything changed. I became deeply attached to the brother and sister whom I had wanted to kill. This the Medicine accomplished for me.

John Rave[44]

Ordeal

Taking Peyote is a test; an ordeal. We do not take it for fun. We suffer. We regard a Peyote meeting as tough — almost as self-torture. We think of it as a kind of stationary pilgrimage that replicates the bitter road of war, starvation, and loneliness that our heroes had to travel before Peyote redeemed them.

Anonymous[45]

An experience of Peyote is one you remember all your life. When it comes around in a meeting, you take four spoonfuls. First you become tired, and then you become relaxed — relaxed but suffering, because you're there for ten to twelve hours and the entire night becomes a matter of dealing with the space around you and how your body sits. Which is to say, you learn by looking. You watch how the old timers sit, as if relaxed. They hardly move. Myself, I could hardly sit still. It's learning through watching and participating.

Tom Cook, St. Regis Mohawk

The drink is as bitter as the death I am awaiting.

Quanah Parker[46]

Peyote isn't easy on you like the Bible is. It will be hard on you if you aren't ready for it. We call using it for kicks shooting yourself, because Peyote is loaded and can backfire.

You have to prepare to use it. You must purify yourself, be

free of alcohol and be in a humble, benevolent state of mind.

Anonymous[47]

Bereavement and Death

Many people have gone on the path of this life and beyond. Our altar, which is in the shape of a mound, is Mother Earth where you come from and where you return. It is the same as the Biblical passage, "from dust to dust." As you eat Peyote, the altar becomes a grave into which many a man has gone.

Lawrence Hunter[48]

My grandmother wanted her Last Sacraments. They were going to call a minister, but she said she wanted them in the Peyote way. William Black Bear gave her four Peyote balls, and my father sang four songs. They said the Lord's Prayer, and she said Amen and breathed her last breath.   *Eva Gap*[49]

The year the submarine *Thresher* went down, our Roadman poked fire for George Gap, who was a Navy man. That year they had a memorial service at Denby over at Sitting Hawk's place. In the morning Joe Sierra prayed for those people who went down in the *Thresher*. That morning, instead of the eagle he laid an anchor on our altar. That was real good, I thought. He was really wise.   *Beatrice Weasel Bear*[50]

Responses to The Supreme Court's Outlawing of Peyote

BEFORE THE AMERICAN INDIAN RELIGIOUS FREEDOM ACT AMENDMENTS OF 1994 WERE PASSED

My name is Alfred Leo Smith, and I am a member of the Klamath Nation.

In 1985 my employment with an alcohol and drug treatment agency in Roseburg, Oregon, was terminated. One Friday afternoon my supervisor called me into his office and asked if I was a member of the Native American Church. I said I was, and he asked if I used the drug, peyote. I said, "No, but I do take the holy sacrament." He told me not to, that it was illegal, and then checked up on me on Monday, asking if I had taken the drug during the Saturday night ceremony. Again I said no, but that I had partaken of the sacrament. So he said I left him no alternative but to fire me.

I applied for unemployment compensation but I was denied. On April 17, 1990, in a decision that carries my name, *Employment Division of Oregon v. Smith*, the Supreme Court of the United States backed up that denial by ruling that "the free exercise of religion" clause in the Constitution of the United States doesn't extend to the Native American Church in this situation.

I feel that I have been no more than a pawn in this whole affair, but reflecting on the extent that it has rallied my people and others to the defense of their religious rights, I feel good now to have had a part in it. I'm seventy-five and enthusiastic about continuing my journey back to the Creator from whom I came.

Alfred Leo Smith, Klamath Nation

As I understand things, the Constitution of the United States guarantees that we all have certain human rights, among which is the right to worship as we deem right. But it has worked out that everybody seems to have these rights except Indians. That's the part I don't understand.

John Emhoola, Kiowa Tribe

When I enlisted in the Army in 1987 my people had a prayer ceremony for me. And when I was sent to Germany, and later to Saudi Arabia, they prayed for my safe return.

I did return safely and received an honorable discharge in 1991. But then my life went downhill and I went for alcohol. I grew apart from my family to the point where I couldn't even talk to them, but then I realized that I needed help and talked to my father. He suggested a prayer service in our Church and I said, "Prayer brought me home safe from the war; I'm all for it." So we went ahead and arranged one as soon as possible and it turned my life around 180 degrees. It helped me especially as a single parent, for I wanted everything for my son, and after that meeting I sobered up and got a job again.

Now I find that my Church is in trouble. When I entered military service I took an oath. I raised my right hand and said, "I am an American fighting in the armed forces which protect our country and our way of life. I am prepared to give my life in its defense." I lived up to that. I laid my life on the line, in Operation Desert Shield/Desert Storm and the highway of death.

I think I deserve the right to my religion — the right for it to continue the way we want it to without outside interference.

Troy Nakai, Navajo

It's hypocritical, this Supreme Court Decision against our Church. I have many relatives who served in Desert Storm. We prayed for them regularly. One of my cousins, a quiet man who was brought up in our Church, ran one of the computers that fired missiles in that war.

For him to defend his country like that, and then have his country forbid him to pray — pray in the way he believes, which is the only way you can pray sincerely — it's not right.

Loretta Afraid-of-Bear Cook

The Native American Church is the only true Church of our people. It is an intertribal, multi-language network that joins hands to bring our people together.

As President of the ninety-one chapters of that Church in Navajoland, I know our history well, and it shows a recurrent pattern. When we want to pray, we have to look up to see if someone is watching us. That means that we pray in fear. We'd like to be free of shadows that follow us.

The Smith Decision of the Supreme Court may have come at the right time. Had it come later, we might not have had the unity to stand together to protest it.

Robert Billie White Horse

AFTER THE ACT WAS PASSED

I have suggested to the President of our Church that we write a thank-you letter to the Supreme Court for its 1990 decision against us.

It could say:

We were unhappy about it at the time, but in the long run you did us a favor. With all the problems that seem to be coming our way, we were beginning to wonder if we should continue to worship in our Native American ways. You sent shockwaves through our Church. The threat your decision posed — that it might do us in — made us realize how much the Church means to us. It mobilized our energies. We went to work, and in four years won back our rights through Congress.

So thank you, Supreme Court. Your blow against us turned out to be a blessing in disguise.

Elmer L. Blackbird, Omaha

NOTES

1. Quoted in James S. Slotkin, "Menomini Peyotism. A Study of Individual Variation in a Primary Group with a Homogeneous Culture," *Transactions of the American Philosophical Society* 42 (1952), 571.
2. Quoted in Omer C. Stewart, *Peyote Religion: A History* (Norman: University of Oklahoma Press, 1987), 157.
3. Quoted in Slotkin, "Menomini Peyotism," 606.
4. Paul B. Steinmetz, *Bible, Pipe and Peyote among the Oglala Lakota* (Knoxville, Tenn.: University of Tennessee Press, 1990), 100.
5. *Ibid.*, 100.
6. Peggy V. Beck and A. I. Walters, *The Sacred Ways of Knowledge, Sources of Life* (Tsaile, Ariz.: Navajo Community College Press, 1977), 233.
7. Steinmetz, *Bible*, 100.
8. Walter W. Snyder, "The Native American Church: Its Origin, Ritual, Doctrine, and Ethic," *Bulletin of the Oklahoma Anthropological Society* 18 (1969): 16.

9. Warren I. D'Azevedo, *Straight with the Medicine. Narratives of Washoe Followers of the Tipi Way* (Reno: University of Nevada, 1978), 13.
10. Slotkin, "Menomini Peyotism," 632.
11. *Ibid.*, 634. Paraphrased.
12. David F. Aberle, *The Peyote Religion among the Navajo* (Chicago: Adeline, 1966), 6; and John H. Laney, "The Peyote Movement: An Introduction," *Spring* (1972): 129. Edited.
13. George Dearborn & Louise Spindler, *Dreamers without Power. The Menomini Indians* (New York: Holt, Reinhart and Winston, 1971), 96.
14. Vincenzo Petrullo, *The Diabolic Root. A Study of Peyotism, the New Indian Religion, among the Delawares* (Philadelphia: University of Pennsylvania Press, 1934), 35; and Paul Radin, *The Winnebago Tribe* (Lincoln: University of Nebraska Press, 1971), 351. Edited.
15. Aberle, *Peyote Religion*, 166.
16. Slotkin, "Menomini Peyotism.", 582.
17. Henry and Lloyd Old Coyote, "The Sacramental Use of Peyote," *Absaroka* (March 1969): 4.
18. Steinmetz, *Bible*, 102.
19. *Ibid.*, 103-4.
20. *Ibid.*, 104.
21. *Ibid.*, 105.
22. *Ibid.*, 106.
23. Morris E. Opler, "A Description of a Tonkawa Peyote Meeting Held in 1902," *American Anthropologist*, 41 (1939): 437.
24. William E. Bittle, "The Peyote Ritual: Kiowa-Apache," *Bulletin of the Oklahoma Anthropological Society*, 2 (1954): 76.
25. Slotkin, "Menomini Peyotism," 624.
26. *Ibid.*, 616.
27. Paul Radin, "The Religious Experiences of an American Indian," *Eranos-Jahrbuch*, 18 (1950): 262.
28. Steinmetz, *Bible*, 100.
29. Beck & Walters, *Sacred Ways*, 233.
30. Slotkin, "Menomini Peyotism," 615.

31. *Ibid.*, 629.
32. "Peyote Origin Myth," as told to Omer C. Stewart, 1938, mss; and Eve Ball, "Peyote Priest," *Frontier Times*, 40 (1966): 7.
33. Slotkin, "Menomini Peyotism," 636.
34. *Ibid.*, 629.
35. *Ibid.*, 590.
36. Steinmetz, *Bible*, 99.
37. Navajo Tribal Council, "Minutes of Meeting, 1-3 June, 1954," mimeograph, Centre for New Religious Movements, Selly Oak Colleges, Birmingham, England.
38. Steinmetz, *Bible*, 105.
39. *Ibid.*, 111.
40. Slotkin, "Menomini Peyotism," 606. Paraphrased.
41. Steinmetz, *Bible*, 110.
42. *Ibid.*
43. Albert H. Kneale, *Indian Agent. An Autobiographical Sketch* (Caldwell, Idaho: Caxton Printers, 1950), 212.
44. Radin, "Religious Experiences," 258.
45. Aberle, *Peyote Religion*, 9; and Haniel Long, *Piñon Country* (New York: Duell, Sloan & Pearce, 1941), 234. Adapted.
46. Alice Marriott & Carol K. Rachlin, *American Indian Mythology* (New York: New American Library, 1968), 209.
47. Warren L. D'Azevedo, *Straight with the Medicine*, 37-8; and C. S. Simmons, "The Peyote Road: An Exegesis of the Religious and Mystic Rites of the North American Indians," Smithsonian Institution, Bureau of American Ethnology Archives, No. 2537 (1918): 7. Adapted.
48. Steinmetz, *Bible*, 101.
49. *Ibid.*, 100-1.
50. *Ibid.*, 105.

"Peyote Leader," pochois print, by Stephen Mopope. Courtesy Oklahoma Indian Arts Gallery.

2

The Peyote Ceremony

Phil Cousineau and Gary Rhine

For thousands of years the indigenous peoples of North America have been making long pilgrimages to gather Peyote, a cactus plant they believe is holy Medicine placed here on earth by the Creator to heal them and give them spiritual guidance.

In describing the mythic origins of the sacred Medicine that has been at the center of his life, Truman Dailey, a ninety-six-year-old Otoe-Missouri Peyote Roadman tells how the Ancestors thought of the Creator as a kind of artist. "The Old Folks say that he gathered things and set up the world, but there was nobody around to see and enjoy it."

When the Creator realized there was no one around to appreciate the world's beauty, he made the first people, the Ancestors. Believing that a tremendous spirit must have been behind their strange and mysterious surroundings, the Ancestors decided to give thanks and to pray. But soon their world became troubled. The Creator thought, "My children are going to need help. They're going to need something to help them understand."

And that is why, as Truman tells the story, "the Creator put a little extra in the holy Peyote Medicine, and when our people got hold of it they made it the center of a beautiful ceremony."

In this one humble story, retold by a man who has been

A garden of Peyote cactus plants. Courtesy of Kifaru Productions.

praying with the Medicine for over ninety years, we find several themes that are at the heart of the Peyote ceremony: praise, spiritual guidance, prayer, thanksgiving, and a means for native peoples to understand the paradox of suffering at the heart of the miraculous gift of life. Through the sacred Medicine, the Creator helped his people to see the road they must walk together, the Peyote road, the path of the spiritual life.

The origin stories about Peyote converge on the Great Plains of the United States in the early 1890s, the convulsive era of forced settlement of many Indian tribes. Many of the time-honored ways of worship were being banished. In those spiritually troubled times, the use of Peyote was formalized into beautiful ceremonies under the inspiration of Medicine men like the Comanche Quanah Parker and John Wilson of the Caddo tribe. In the gradual diffusion of the Peyote religion throughout North America, two forms of the ceremony diverged into distinct practices known as the Comanche Half Moon and the Wilson Big Moon, or Cross Fire, ceremonies. Both of these forms fused ancient Mexican, Plains Indian, and Christian themes so effectively that they have maintained their basic structure for more than 120 years.

From its earliest days, the Peyote ceremony has consisted of an all-night prayer meeting in a tepee, lodge, or hogan around a crescent moon–shaped mound of earth, a sacred fire, and a special "Grandfather" Peyote button. Around these sacred elements, the water drum, gourd rattle, and staff are passed while Peyote songs are sung, prayers are offered, sacred tobacco is smoked, cedar is burned, and Peyote is ingested. At dawn there is a water ceremony followed by a ritual breakfast of corn, fruit, and meat. Finally, the morning sun is greeted with hands raised to the heavens and thanks given to the Creator.

The appeal of these gatherings ranges from the curative powers of Peyote, which are legendary, to the cohesive social force of the meetings, but no list can exhaust their hold on the people who take part in the rite. Peyote is usually referred to as "Medicine," an elusive term that carries both pharmacological and mystical connotations. In 1896, the Smithsonian anthropologist James Mooney was profoundly moved by the ceremonies he was privileged to witness. "It may be said," he reported, "that the Indians regard the Peyote as a panacea in Medicine, a source of inspiration, and the key which opens the glories of another world."

What happens during the long night of a Peyote ceremony that can open a participant's heart to the mysteries of another world? What is behind the rich symbolism of the different rituals that comprise the prayer meeting? What is meant by the Peyote road?

Initiating the Ceremony

Tradition decrees that a Peyote meeting be instigated by a sponsor who presents the Roadman — the leader of the all-night ceremony — with sacred tobacco. There are a multitude of reasons why someone might propose a meeting: to celebrate a birth or wedding, to mourn a death, to bless children before their return to school, to avert illness or evil, to cure someone, to pray for the safe return of a relative from a tour in the armed services, or to honor a great achievement, invariably while seeking the Creator's help and guidance. Whatever the express purpose of the meeting, it is always faithful to the Peyote way of life, which includes curing, sobriety, Christian ideals, and the preservation of time-honored traditional ways.

A meeting time is determined. Often it is a Saturday night, "in deference," Mooney wrote, "to the white man's idea of Sunday as a sacred day and a day of rest." Or the meeting may be timed to a holiday, or take place simply, as the Taos Indians say, "when someone thinks it's time."

After the sacred tobacco is accepted by the Roadman and a time is agreed upon, the tepee is raised during the afternoon preceding the ceremony. The elders say that it should be built as neatly and as perfectly as possible, in order to be "presentable to the Lord," as Otoe-Missouri Roadman Johnny White Cloud said in the 1993 documentary film, *The Peyote Road*. The Winnebago Roadman Reuben Snake used to say that the canvas or hide of the tepee should be drawn so taut around the lodge poles that if you flick it with your finger you will hear a note that vibrates in the key of C major!

Once the tepee is erected, firewood is stacked on the east side of the lodge for the Fireman to use during the long night. A shallow fire hole is dug in the center of the lodge or tepee, around which an altar is fashioned into a crescent-shaped mound of earth a few inches high, that opens to the sacred east. Anthropologist Weston La Barre noted that the crescent symbolizes the mountain range where the "Peyote Woman" discovered the sacred plant. Along the top of the mound a thin line is grooved from end to end, symbolizing the Peyote road. This line represents the road of life "from birth at one end to the crest of maturity, and then downward to old age and death at the other end," La Barre wrote. It is this symbolic

Navajo Roadman's sacred objects for Peyote Ceremony. Photograph by Marcia Keegan.

Kenneth Begay, Navajo Roadman. Photograph by Marcia Keegan.

road that participants are asked to concentrate on during the ceremony in the belief that it will lead their thoughts and prayers to the Creator. It is also the inspiration for the name given to the Roadman who is believed to have the power to lead people on the spiritual path.

Reuben Snake explained in *The Peyote Road* that the crescent moon shape symbolizes "the path we take when we come from the spirit world and we start down this road of life on the earthly plane." When asked what the road meant to those in the Native American Church, Johnny White Cloud said that Peyote religion is more than a ritual; it is a way of life that "promotes family stability, sobriety, self-sufficiency, and brotherly love."

As twilight falls, the leaders of the ceremony and the participants, today both men and women, quietly assemble. The principal roles are performed by the Roadman, who has spent years memorizing every intricate detail of the all-night vigil; the Drum Chief, who sits on the right of the Roadman and accompanies the singing; the Cedarman, who sits on the Roadman's left and places cedar on the fire; the Fireman or Fire Chief, who sits on the opposite side of the circle next to the door and tends the fire through the long night; and the Water Woman, who brings blessed water into the meeting at dawn.

Despite the intricate details of the ten- to twelve-hour ceremony, there is no formal teaching or learning of the rituals through books, schools, or lectures. Instead, as Omer Stewart pointed out in his classic study, *Peyote Religion: A History*, "the ritual is always learned by one man from another and by repeated attendance at many meetings for the purpose of learning how it should be done." Through careful observation, the

"Peyote Meeting," pochois print, by Stephen Mopope. Courtesy Oklahoma
Indian Arts Gallery.

sequence of events, the songs, the drumming rhythms, and the prayers are memorized and work their way into the unconscious mind.

The Preparation

When all is readied, the Fireman enters the tepee and ignites the fire. The Roadman quiets himself; he focuses on the purpose of the evening's gathering and blows an eaglebone whistle as he leads all the participants on a ritual circuit around the outside of the sacred lodge. Then, one by one, all enter through the door that has been carefully positioned to the east, each taking his or her place inside until the circle is complete. All sit crosslegged on blankets or carpets that have been spread on the ground, which is sometimes strewn with wild sage. The Roadman sits at the westernmost point of the tepee, opposite the Fireman who sits to the north of the flap door.

When everyone has settled into place, the Roadman arranges his ceremonial instruments reverently and attentively. From out of his personal instrument box or case, he removes his gourd rattle, staff, feathers, eagle wingbone whistle, corn shucks and tobacco, and bags for Peyote, cedar, and sage incense. Each item has its own special purpose and unique symbolism. As one Roadman is fond of saying, "Each is a work of love because we love this way of life."

Depending on the tribal tradition, the elaborately carved and beaded staff — often with a shock of dyed horsehair — can represent the staff of life, a walking stick, the savior's staff, or a hunting spear. According to an Otoe-Missouri Roadman, "Some of these staffs are fashioned in the form of a spear or a

Peyote Fan used in ceremony. Courtesy of Kifaru Productions.

lance that we would use in the buffalo hunt, and some are fashioned like a bow that we would take out into the wilderness to provide for our families and to protect our villages and our way of life. So in the Peyote meeting, when we use the staff and sing with it, we are looking for something good, and for protection and a good life for our families."

The decorated gourd or Peyote rattle is also intricately beaded, and features a shock of horsehair. According to the Wichita, it represents both the world and the sun. The beads inside the "world" are people talking, while the outer beadwork represents the things of this world.

Johnny White Cloud quotes the Twenty-third Psalm to explain the depths of association carried by the sacramental instruments. "All the days of my life I will fear no evil, for thy rod and thy staff will comfort me." The instruments and the songs are the comfort of those who follow the Peyote way.

The prayer fan is made from of the feathers of sacred birds and is believed to have the power to send prayers to the Creator through the smoke hole at the top of the tepee. The Roadman's fan is greatly honored; it features the twelve feathers of the great eagle, and is used for healing. The fan also symbolizes the twelve months of the year, and (where there have been Christian infusions) the wings of birds mentioned in the Bible's Book of Revelations. Other prayer fans may be fashioned out of the feathers of hawks, waterbirds, and macaws.

The eaglebone whistle is used at midnight and again at dawn, and is believed by some to echo the cry of the eagle in search of water. The reverence paid to the eagle is due to its being the bird that flies the highest, circling higher and higher into the heavens until it can be heard but not seen. The

Winnebago Peyote Roadman Reuben Snake, singing traditional Peyote songs with staff, fan, and gourd rattle. Courtesy of Kifaru Productions.

eagle is believed to be the only bird that can see where the Creator lives.

The water drum, which is used to drive the Peyote songs, creates the rhythm which is the ceremony's soul. The drum is tied with ropes that crisscross to form a pattern that is associated with the Morning Star in the night sky. According to the Kiowas, the four coals placed inside the drum represent water, rain, thunder, and lightning, and the drumming itself is meant to evoke the sound of thunder. It is also widely believed that being inside the tepee represents being inside the womb of the Mother, and the drum is the sound of the fetal heartbeat within her womb.

Finally, there is a special Peyote button, said to be the Chief, or Grandfather Peyote, which the Roadman will reverently place on the altar. Sometimes a woven altar cloth will have been placed there to receive it.

Once the instruments have been spread between the Roadman and the altar, the Cedarman throws a handful of cedar onto the fire and for a few moments the deep aroma of the forest fills the lodge. The Roadman then passes the water drum, staff, and fan through the cedar smoke for purification. In Half Moon ceremonies, tobacco and cornhusk rolling paper for cigarettes may also be distributed, as they are in many other native rituals. When tobacco is included, it and the cornhusks are passed clockwise around the tepee. Each participant rolls his or her own cigarette for a ceremonial smoke. While smoking and praying, many participants will use their free hands to pull some of the sacred smoke over their bodies and end by resting the hand on the heart, signifying that they are "taking the prayers to heart."

The Opening Prayers

The Roadman opens the meeting by humbly reminding everyone why they have gathered. He might ask the sponsor to say a few words about the reason for the assembly. Then the Roadman initiates the communal smoke in which each person prays to the Creator while gazing at the altar and its fire. After the smoke, the Fireman collects the husks and carefully places them around the edge of the altar.

As the Roadman raises his voice in prayer, the Cedarman passes the holy Medicine around the circle of participants in a clockwise direction. It can be in the form of cactus tea, dry powder, or raw buttons. Each individual takes the portion he thinks will benefit him most.

Once the opening rituals have concluded, the Roadman lifts his staff and fan with one hand, and his gourd rattle with the other, as he sings the Opening Song. With his gourd rattle shaking in the air, the Chief Drummer pushing him with a rhythm, and the hearts of the assembly focused on the purpose of the meeting, a Roadman can mesmerize the participants with his singing. Most importantly, he focuses the group's attention and prayers on the collective purpose of the meeting, "so their minds fuse into one thought," as Reuben Snake has said.

As Quanah Parker, the last Comanche chief and one of the first Peyote missionaries, said, "The white man goes into his church and talks about God. The Indian goes into his tepee and talks to God."

After visiting the Tarahumara in Mexico, the French poet Antonin Artaud wrote that, "Peyote leads the self back to its true source."

His words echo the traditional expectation that the combination of Medicine, singing, drumming, and good intentions will deliver the group's prayers to the Creator with great force.

Loretta Afraid-of-Bear Cook says that one must keep one's mind focused on the reason for the gathering throughout the entire night. "There will come times when you want to pray for your own family, but that should come last. The primary reason that you are in this meeting is because its sponsor is asking for help. That's the true purpose of why you are present."

Sitting Up

While prayers and songs are being raised to the Creator, eyes are either closed in personal contemplation of the Grandfather, or are open, either gazing at the Old Man Peyote button on the altar or at the sacred fire that will reveal his will, for the flames of the fire are "God's tongue talking to us."

The participants sit quietly and as still as possible throughout the long night, offering up their prayers for the reason the meeting was called. The act of sitting still for so long is difficult and often painful. The St. Regis-Mohawk Tom Cook believes that

> the experience of Peyote is one you will remember your entire life. Your body starts to become tired, and then you are relaxed. You relax, but you suffer because you are sitting up in a tepee for ten or twelve hours and the entire evening becomes a matter of how you deal with the space around you and how you sit. You learn by looking. You watch the way the Old Timers sit, as though they are

Peyote practice session with (left to right) Johnny White Cloud, Hayna Brown, actor Rodney Grant, and Reuben Snake. Courtesy of Kifaru Productions.

at total peace. They are hardly moving. You learn the Old Ways by listening and imitating. As the fire consumes your attention, you become contemplative. The old and the new, the ancient and modern, come together. And throughout, the drum is pushing everything toward the eastern sky.

Native American ceremonial acts are typically performed in fours. The Peyote circle is no exception as each singer sings four Peyote songs before passing the staff, fan, and rattle to the person on his left. He may choose the Drum Chief or another drummer to accompany him in his singing. Some choose not to sing. When the staff comes to them, they respectfully acknowledge its sacredness, as well as that of the Water Drum that follows, before passing these items to the next in the circle.

As midnight approaches, the Roadman lets the participants know that this is the time when they may take out their personal ceremonial rattles and fans for use in the rest of the ceremony. Great pride is invested in these instruments. Often they have been personally crafted, or are treasured family heirlooms.

The Midnight Ceremony

Around midnight, the Fireman brings in the ceremonial pail of water. He prays over the water and passes it through the cedar smoke before placing it in front of the Roadman. The Roadman, using his eaglebone whistle, marks the surface of the water with two perpendicular lines in the form of a Medicine Wheel Cross. He then touches each of the four quadrants of the surface of the water with the eaglebone whistle, which honors the four sacred directions. After that, he dips his prayer fan into the water four times. Following each dip, he flicks water in the four directions of the tepee as libations or ritual offerings. He then uses the water to bless each of his own instruments, the Grandfather Peyote button, and himself before he passes the water around the circle.

Once the water ceremony is complete, the Roadman sings four songs and passes the Staff once again to his left, resuming the cycle of four songs per person. While the deep tones of the prayers and the plaintive melodies of the songs continue and the staff makes its way around the circle, the Roadman slips quietly outside. In the shadow of the firelit tepee, he blows four times on his eaglebone whistle, a ritual gesture that in some traditions symbolizes the eagle's scream. According to the Comanches, the whistle announces to the four directions that a sacred meeting is in progress, while the Shawnees blow it "on account of the four different winds." A Cheyenne hero and Cross Fire practitioner, Sweet Medicine, held that the purpose of the midnight whistle is "to notify all things in all directions that we are having a meeting here in the center of the cross, and to call the Great Power to be with us while we drink his Medicine so that he can hear our prayers."

When the Roadman returns to the lodge he may announce an opportunity for participants to take a short break during which they may stretch or relieve themselves. When they return, the drumming, singing, and praying resumes.

As the night marches on, the holy Medicine is passed around the circle. At the end of each round of songs, the Cedarman says a prayer for the purpose of the meeting. This "main prayer" introduces a moment of utmost seriousness, for it helps to refocus the participants' attention on the central

*Ceremonial Fireman (L) and Water Woman (R) about to enter tepee.
Courtesy of Kifaru Productions.*

Rodney Grant lifts his hand in thanks to the Creator. Courtesy of Kifaru Productions.

reason for the meeting. Once the Cedarman has finished his prayer, he stands and drops cedar onto the fire. Then, making his way slowly around the tepee, he fans cedar smoke onto each person. When this has been completed, he will often invite a respected elder in the group to pray.

In the depth of the night the Roadman may perform a healing ritual for someone who is ill. Others may report on the conditions of absent ones who could use the help of prayers by the group. Confessions erupt in these deepest hours of the night, and a mood of humility and compassion becomes almost palpable. There is no shame or judgment if someone breaks down in tears, crying out to the Powers for forgiveness, or for a blessing, or for a directive that could make a vital change in his life. Others, including the Roadman, will commend him for his sincerity and "good words." The intense atmosphere at such moments is often reminiscent of the traditional Vision Quest.

And so it goes: words, prayers, drumming, and singing until the first birds are heard outdoors and the dawning light of morning becomes visible through the canvas of the tepee.

The Morning Water Call Song

When daylight clearly shows through the tepee's canvas the Roadman lifts his voice in the Dawn or Water Song. On some occasions he will again blow his eaglebone whistle four times in tribute to the four directions, the four races, the four seasons, and the four generations that occupy the tepee. The Water Woman — who is the wife or another relative of the Roadman, and who represents the Peyote Woman who discovered the sacred Medicine — then carries in the pail of morning water. She sits across from the Roadman, then prays in a way that brings the attention of the assembly back to the concerns of the sponsor, though she may also add prayers for other friends and relatives and will invariably thank the Great Spirit for his creation. The pail is then passed around the circle for all to slake their thirst.

As the water makes its way around the circle, participants have the opportunity to speak. In some traditions anyone may speak when the pail arrives, while in other traditions this opportunity is reserved for certain attendees whom the Roadman honors by inviting them to "say a few words."

Once the water ceremony is completed, the Water Woman (along with several helpers) brings in the morning meal. Ceremonial vessels containing parched corn, hashed and sweetened beef, and stewed fruit are placed in a straight line between the fire and the doorway, and are blessed with cedar smoke. When all is in order, the Roadman and his assistant sing four more songs accompanied by the drum and gourd rattle.

As the food is being passed around the circle, the Roadman may deliver an inspirational morning talk. While focusing for a final time on the purpose of the meeting, he will typically include parables from, and references to, old Indian Ways. In the Cross Fire ceremony an appropriate reading from the Bible may also figure. While this is going on, the Fireman sculpts the embers and ashes of the fire into marvelous shapes of waterbirds, sunbursts, sun eagles, hummingbirds, buffalo heads, or a cross.

When the rays of the rising sun slip through the tepee's door and strike the fire, it is considered time for the next hymn, the Quitting Song, which is sung with the full force of the night's vigil behind it, Hayna Brown, a Winnebago, reports that his lifelong friend Reuben Snake always said, "It is not the Quitting, but the Moving-On Song, because we are in no way quitting. We are moving on!"

As the last notes of the song and drum fade away, the Roadman begins to carefully store his ceremonial instruments, wrapping his rattle, fan, and Grandfather Peyote in decorative protective coverings before storing them in his personal case. The Fireman carries the Roadman's case out of the tepee and the participants follow him to "welcome the sun." Weston La Barre sees in this reversal of roles, with the Fireman now taking the lead, the symbolism of "the first shall be last, and the last shall be first."

As each person exits the tepee into the crisp morning air, it is customary for all to raise their hands to the four directions of the heavens in gratitude. This longstanding practice is not confined to mornings that follow church meetings. Every day, Indians say, "you should get out of your bed before the sun rises, go outdoors, and with hands outstretched toward the Creator, give thanks for the new day that has been given to you."

With greetings, handshakes, embraces, and good feelings for having "sat up" together, participants stretch, greet one another as "Brother" and "Sister", and visit amicably. Soon everyone reenters the tepee for a leisurely breakfast that the host's family has prepared. This gives the Roadman the opportunity to invite members of the circle to express their feelings. These heartfelt sentiments are usually expressed simply. "I want to greet each and everyone from the doorway in to the doorway out," someone may begin. Often, a speaker will address each person in the circle individually, if only to say good morning, affirm a family relationship, or express gratitude to those who have travelled a great distance to participate. Invariably the words are sincere, and the prevailing mood is one of humility, respect, and affection that phases into family love. The constant backdrop to these moving expressions is gratitude to the Creator.

With these feelings stirring within them, the participants say their goodbyes and head for home.

"The Sacraments," acrylic, by Mirae Creeping Bear. Courtesy Oklahoma
Indian Arts Gallery.

3

Pharmacology, Legal Classification, and the Issue of Substance Abuse

Edward F. Anderson

Our current drug crisis is a tragedy born of a phony system of classification. For reasons that are little more than accidents of history, we have divided a group of nonfood substances into two categories: items purchasable for supposed pleasure (such as alcohol), and illicit drugs. The categories were once reversed. Opiates were legal in America before the Harrison Narcotics Act of 1914, and members of the Women's Christian Temperance Union, who campaigned against alcohol during the day, drank their valued "women's tonics" at night, products laced with laudanum (tincture of opium).

I could abide — though I would still oppose — our current intransigence if we applied the principle of total interdiction to all harmful drugs. But how can we possibly defend our current policy based on a dichotomy that encourages us to view one class of substances as a preeminent scourge while the two most dangerous and life-destroying substances by far, alcohol and tobacco, form a second class advertised in neon on every street corner of urban America? And why, moreover, should heroin be viewed with horror while chemical cognates that are no different from heroin than lemonade is from iced tea perform work of enormous compassion by relieving the pain of terminal cancer patients in their last days?

Stephen J. Gould[1]

 At the heart of the controversy over the Native American Church is its central, sacramental substance, the peyote cactus. Members of the NAC consider it "God's flesh;" many European immigrants view it as a dangerous drug, which to Native Americans is analogous to calling the wine in the Christian eucharist booze. Members believe that it helps them cope with life's problems; opponents charge that it is dangerous.

Since misinformation and prejudice fuel this controversy, a knowledge of the facts can upgrade the level of the debate. This chapter begins by dealing with the chemistry of peyote, together with scientific findings regarding its effects on the human body, especially the brain. It then proceeds to summarize what is known about its consequences for human behavior. Does peyote, on balance, help people in the living of their lives, or does it induce asocial behavior? Is it more bane or boon, especially when ingested in the context of the Native American Church and its rites? Finally, the chapter questions the rationality of the way peyote is currently classified by the federal government.

Pharmacology:
Peyote's Effects on the Body and Mind

Peyote belongs to the cactus genus *Lophophora*, of which there are two species: *L. williamsii* and *L. diffusa*.[2] *L. williamsii* is the most widespread of the two species, ranging from west and south Texas into the Mexican state of San Luis Potosí. The vegetation of this area is Tamaulipan Thorn Forest and Chihuahuan Desert. *L. diffusa* is found only in an isolated portion of the Chihuahuan Desert in the Mexican state of Querétaro. Native Americans use only *L. williamsii* for religious and medicinal purposes because of its chemical makeup. It contains more than fifty-five alkaloids, including the well-known psychoactive alkaloid mescaline. *L. diffusa*, on the other hand, has fewer alkaloids and lacks mescaline.[3]

While there is incontrovertible evidence that Native Americans have been using peyote for more than 1,000 years, its use probably extends much farther into the past.[4] Both historical and current accounts point to *L. williamsii* as the species that has been used, and it seems clear that this is due to the mescaline it contains. Another cactus, known as the San Pedro cactus (*Echinopsis pachanoi*), contains comparable amounts of mescaline and is used by Peruvians in ways similar to those of Mexican Native Americans.[5]

There are persistent claims for the curative powers of peyote, but the primary reason for its use seems to be its profound effects on the human mind. Chemically speaking, these effects are due to the psychoactive alkaloid mescaline. Alkaloids are derived from amino acids, and are defined chemically as cyclic organic compounds which contain nitrogen in a negative oxidation state.[6] They are found in plants, animals, fungi, bacteria, and protists, but are particularly widespread in the flowering plants. The function of alkaloids in plants is unclear. Previously, they were thought to be reservoirs for nitrogen or waste products of the plant's metabolic reactions, but recent studies suggest that alkaloids may protect the plant from predators (herbivores) and parasites. They may also serve as growth regulators.[7]

Many alkaloids are not psychoactive, and some psychoactive plants do not contain nitrogen compounds. However, mescaline does contain nitrogen, although some chemists refer to it as a "protoalkaloid" because it does not contain an indole nucleus or ring.

The numerous alkaloids of peyote include both phenylethylamines and isoquinolines. The phenylethylamine mescaline, known chemically as 3,4,5-trimethoxy-B-phenethylamine, is the alkaloid primarily responsible for peyote's effects on the mind. It makes up approximately 1.5 percent of the dry weight of the cactus.[8]

The psychological effects of mescaline, described by numerous researchers,[9] raise the question of how this alkaloid affects the brain. Mescaline, and similar psychoactive agents (such as LSD), alters the action of serotonin, one of the main neurotransmitters within the central nervous system. It seems to act at a post-synaptic serotonin receptor site, specifically of the $5\text{-}HT_2$ subtype.[10]

Peyote's effects can be divided into two stages in which the "hangover precedes the ebriety," if such wording is appropriate in speaking of a plant indigenous peoples consider sacred.[11] In other words, the first phase is dominated by bodily symptoms, whereas mental manifestations come later.

Physical symptoms may range from nausea and vomiting to dizziness, sweating, and headaches. Mental changes, for their part, usually begin with alterations in the way the world is perceived through the senses. Anthropologist J. S. Slotkin's report of the second, or mental, phase of his experience in a Menomini Peyote meeting provides a typical description of these changes.

After midnight I began to notice the effects of the peyote. There were slight, visual effects: the fire was the most beautifully colored I've ever seen, and the shadows cast by the fire flickered in time to the drumming. Auditory effects: I could hear whispers at the other side of the tipi (sharpened acuity), and at first these whispers seemed to come from right behind me. In all, there was much distortion in auditory acuity and direction. Suddenly I realized, as I sat with my eyes closed, that the drumming seemed to be coming from inside of me. I paid some attention to this, and discovered that the distinction between my self and non-self disappeared when I closed my eyes. Puzzled, I explored a little further, and found that my sense of touch was fairly well gone. For instance, I couldn't feel my eyeglasses on my face; I had to touch them with my hand in order to make sure they were on.[12]

Sensory changes of this sort can be the prelude to changes in mood. In a religious context, happy, dreamy feelings bring the conviction that one is blessed. Cognition also changes. Often there is a sense of seeing more deeply into the nature of things than one normally does. Visions can appear. In secular terms these are fantasies or hallucinations, though in the strict sense of the word they are not the latter, a point to which I shall return. The experience lasts for eight to ten hours.

Native Americans may ingest from three to more than a dozen peyote "buttons" (the fresh or dry tops of the cactus) in the all-night ceremony. Some may take up to thirty "buttons" during the night, but this is unusual. Thirty buttons would contain about 500 milligrams (0.5 gram) of mescaline, which introduces the issue of overdose and possibility of substance abuse.

The Issue of Substance Abuse

The phrase "substance abuse" refers to the excessive use of drugs without medical justification, which is characterized by the somatic or behavioral toll that outweighs the reason for taking the drug, be it euphoria, sleep, pain relief, or other desired effects.

To begin with the most extreme of these tolls, there have been no proven human fatalities from peyote. Studies of the lethal dose of mescaline on laboratory animals show that they have varying sensibilities. The rat's lethal dose is 132 milligrams per kilogram of body weight, whereas that of the guinea pig is 328. The dog is by far the most sensitive of the animals that have been tested; 54 milligrams per kilogram of its body weight will kill it.[13] As for humans, up to 8,000 milligrams — ten times the typical ingestion at a Peyote meeting — have been taken by human experimental subjects without apparent toxic reactions.[14]

There is a report of one case in which someone drank a cup of peyote tea and within a few hours died of cardiopulmonary arrest, but the autopsy showed that the person suffered from severe alcoholic hepatitis and actually had a very low level of mescaline in his system. The peyote may have caused violent vomiting, which, in turn, may have caused internal bleeding that led to death. A second reported fatality concerned a young man in California who climbed a steep hill near the ocean and leaped off it as if attempting a swan dive. He fell 200 meters to his death. The subsequent autopsy showed high levels of mescaline in his blood system,[15] but as nothing is known of the man's history or emotional state when he took the drug, no clear conclusion can be drawn from this incident.

Peyote appears to cause no chromosome damage. Oscar Janiger, reporting for a team of scientists who researched the matter, gives this report:

Our concern was to see if the repeated use of peyote over time would produce any changes in the body, particularly its chromosomes. The idea of using a native population was very appealing, since some tribes have used it for generations under prescribed circumstances. The Huichol Indians suggested themselves. Some of their tribes use it regularly, and have a complex, sacramental relation to it. We used as our control a group of Huichol who lived some miles away from our experimental group. This gave us two groups with similar life styles but differing in the matter we were researching.

Fifty-seven Huichol Indians with a lifelong individual history (and a 1,600-year cultural tradition) of ingestion of peyote were compared with 50 Huichol Indian controls and ten laboratory controls for effects on lymphocyte chromosomes. The frequency of abnormalities in the experimental and control groups did not differ significantly. No significant chromosomal aberrations were apparent among the peyote- and nonpeyote-using Huichol Indians. The lack of hereditary cytogenetic abnormalities in the experimental population group supports the conclusion that 1,600 years of peyote use has not adversely affected the 'cytogenetic pool.'[16]

As for addiction, a significant study by M. H. Seevers shows that peyote is clearly not addicting. Using an index of "addicting liability," Stevens found alcohol to be the most addictive (with an index of 21), followed by barbiturates (with an index of 18). These were followed by opium and its derivatives (16), cocaine (14), and marijuana (8). Peyote was lowest on the list with an "addicting liability" of only one. The only evidence cited for including it on the scale at all was that some subjects showed a slightly increased tolerance during the test period.[17]

The behavior changes resulting from peyote use are more difficult to measure, but appear to be overwhelmingly (if not entirely) to the good, at least when they arise in an institutionalized religious context. A number of testimonials to the benefits it has accorded members of the Native American Church appear in Chapter One of this book. Here I shall summarize the verdicts of anthropologists, physicians, and social workers.

Early in this century the Smithsonian Institution sent an anthropologist, James Mooney, to Oklahoma to investigate peyote. He expected his research to yield a negative report, but as all the effects he observed were benign, he turned his energies to getting the substance legalized in the state.

David Aberle, author of *The Peyote Religion among the Navajo* (2nd Ed., University of Oklahoma Press, 1991), found no evidence of addiction to peyote, or any satisfactory evidence of harm from it. On the contrary, "testimony amply supports the existence of spiritual, physical, and psychological benefits in most users."

Emery A. Johnson, M.D., MPH., who for twelve years directed the Indian Health Services, entered this report:

> As a practicing physician for 38 years, I had patients who were active members of the NAC and in no instance did I find any evidence of abuse of peyote.
>
> In a recent computer search of the last ten years of medical literature at the National Library of Medicine, I found no report of abuse of peyote in the sacraments of the NAC.
>
> Within the context of the Church, rather than a drug of abuse, peyote is actually used in the treatment of other substances.[18]

One of Dr. Johnson's successors in the office of Director of Indian Health Services, Everett R. Rhodes, M.D., corroborated Dr. Johnson's findings. In a 1990 letter to Reuben Snake, he wrote: "The Native American Church is an important source of strength in efforts to remove the terrible affliction of alcoholism from Indian communities." Two researchers reported "a greater success rate for the Peyotists than for any other agency working with alcoholics" in the part of the Navajo reservation that they studied.[19]

A 1971 statement by the eminent research psychiatrist, Karl T. Menninger, appears to settle this question of whether or not (at least within the context of the NAC) peyote is a substance that invites abuse. After quoting a psychiatrist, Robert Gergman, who had researched the subject, Menninger continued:

> What he says confirms precisely what [the anthropologist] Weston La Barre told me long ago. Peyote is not harmful to these people; it is beneficial, comforting, inspiring, and appears to be spiritually nourishing. It is a better antidote to alcohol than anything the missionaries, white man, the American Medical Association, and the public health services have come up with. It is understandable that these organizations should be a bit envious of the success of this primitive natural native remedy, [for peyote] is a real preventive mental health measure.[20]

LEGAL CLASSIFICATION

One of the most serious legal problems in dealing with plants such as peyote is how they are defined by law. Views and opinions on some drugs have changed as our knowledge of them has increased. For example, during the 1920s and 1930s, when Americans learned about tolerance levels and addiction to drugs, their values changed. Many people came to recognize that narcotics, such as opiates, were no longer just simple medicines but dangerous substances, the use of which needed to be controlled by the government. Unfortunately, society has often lacked accurate scientific facts regarding various drugs and their effects on the human body. Often, law enforcement officers, though acting in good faith, make mistakes which have long-lasting legal consequences. To cite a single example, in the 1930s a man was arrested in Los Angeles for selling heroin and peyote. The police and district attorney reasoned that, since heroin was known to be a dangerous narcotic, peyote must be dangerous, too. Because of their lack of accurate information, they persuaded the California legislature to classify peyote as a narcotic, which it definitely is not according to standard definitions.

That legislative decision brings to focus the issue of how (for purposes of the law) plants such as peyote should be defined and classified. What is a narcotic? What is a dangerous drug? What is a medicine? In the legal sense these can be what a legislature or lawmaking body defines them to be. It is helpful to have scientific definitions of such terms as "narcotic," but until recently none have been generally accepted. With the arrival of more scientifically based (and therefore more generally accepted) definitions, it is now possible for lawmakers to classify drugs more intelligently.

Our English word "narcotic" derives from the Greek, in which *narkē* means "numbness," and *narkōtikos* means "benumbing" or "sleep producing".[21] Most physicians and pharmacists feel that a "narcotic" should be defined on the basis of its physiological effects rather than its social consequences.[22] There is now general agreement that narcotics are the opioids and opioid antagonists,[23] but the issues of physiological tolerance and addiction must enter the picture. Addiction is the condition in which the individual has an overpowering desire or need to continue taking the drug, along with (usually) a psychological (and sometimes physical) dependence on the effects that the drug produces.[24] Tolerance, which is often closely associated with addiction, is typically defined as the condition in which, "after repeated administrations, a given dose of a drug produces a decreasing effect; or conversely, when increasingly larger doses must be administered to obtain the effects observed with the original dose."[25] By these criteria, peyote definitely should not be classified as a narcotic, but some still resist this conclusion.

In 1970 a far-reaching Act was passed by Congress which directed that peyote and its most significant alkaloid, mescaline, be classified as a hallucinogen, not a narcotic. Since the passing of that Act, most states and the federal government have complied.

The word "hallucinogen" does not fit well into the Native American worldview, for error is built into the very meaning of the word* and indigenous peoples credit peyote with more profound deliverances than the senses provide. For example,

---

*Hallucination: (1) the apparent perception of sights, sounds, etc., that are not actually present [which] may occur in certain mental disorders; (2) the imaginary object apparently seen, heard, etc. (*Websters New Universal Unabridged Dictionary*).

the Vision Quest is of major importance in many tribes, especially those of the Plains Indians. Peyote often plays a role in the ritual and Indians do not regard their visions, or what shamans perceive, as hallucinations or psychotomimetic as psychiatrists understand these terms. According to pharmacologists Carl C. Pfeiffer and Henry B. Murphree, hallucinogens "mimic the major psychoses as they occur in man."[26] Stephen Szara divides the hallucinogens into three chemical groups: (1) the phenylethylamine group which includes mescaline and other epinephrine-related substances; (2) the tryptamine group that includes LSD, psilocybin, and related compounds; and (3) a heterogeneous group of non-nitrogenous compounds that have somewhat different psychic and vegetative effects on humans, such as loss of contact with the environment and amnesia during the period of hallucinations.[27] Two examples of this last group would be myristicin, the active substance of nutmeg (*Myristica fragrans*), and the tetrahydrocannabinol alkaloids of *Cannabis sativa* (marijuana).

In an attempt to define the word "hallucinogen" in a way that is less prejudicial to the Native Americans' view, Richard Evans Schultes and Albert Hofmann have proposed this definition:

> *agents which, in nontoxic doses, produce, together or alone, changes in perception, thought and mood, without causing major disturbances of the autonomic nervous system. A variety of hallucinations may be characteristic, especially with high doses. Disorientation, loss or disturbance of memory, excessive impairment of intellectual powers, hyperexcitation or stupor or even narcosis may be experienced only under excessive doses and cannot, there-*

fore, be considered characteristic. Addiction is unknown with these drugs.[28]

This is an improvement, but terminology continues to be a problem. The hallucinogens do not form a single chemical group, but all of them stimulate the peripheral sympathetic nervous system and affect the senses, particularly the visual sense, in major ways.

The federal law dealing with peyote is Public Law 91-513, Comprehensive Drug Abuse Prevention and Control Act of 1970. This law supersedes all other federal legislation dealing with peyote as a drug and establishes five schedules of con-trolled substances, known as Schedules I, II, III, IV, and V. Hallucinogenic substances (which include peyote and mesca-line) are classed as Schedule I substances. Also included in this schedule are opium, LSD, marijuana, and psilocybin. Schedule I substances are defined as having a "high potential for abuse," no currently accepted medical use in the United States, and a lack of "accepted safety" under medical supervi-sion (84 STAT. 1247).

Public Law 91-513 clearly distinguishes the hallucinogens, such as mescaline, peyote, LSD, psilocybin, and marijuana, from the true narcotics which are defined in the law as opium, coca leaves, and opiates. However, peyote and mescaline are still classed as Schedule I controlled substances, and posses-sion is prohibited unless specific permission is obtained or one is a member of the Native American Church. Many experts seriously question the inclusion of peyote in this category, for there is virtually no evidence that human beings have abused it or are likely to do so. Currently, however, there is no effort underway to change its classification.

Section 404 of Public Law 91-513 states that no person can knowingly or intentionally "possess a controlled substance" unless obtained by a prescription or "while acting in the course of [one's] professional practice." Thus simple possession of either peyote or its alkaloid, mescaline, is unlawful, and violators are subject, if convicted, to "imprisonment of not more than one year, a fine of not more than $5,000, or both" (84 STAT 1264).

Of particular significance is 21CFR1307.31 of the law which specifically exempts members of the Native American Church as follows:

> The listing of peyote as a controlled substance in schedule I does not apply to the non-drug use of peyote in bona fide religious ceremonies of the Native American Church, and members of the Native American Church so using peyote are exempt from registration. Any person who manufactures peyote for or distributes peyote to the Native American Church, however, is required to obtain registration annually and to comply with all other requirements of the law.

The federal Comprehensive Drug Abuse Prevention and Control Act of 1970 has stimulated many state legislatures to bring their own laws into agreement with the federal law, so in most cases peyote is now classified as a hallucinogen, not a narcotic. These laws, however, also seem inappropriate considering the large amount of evidence which indicates that peyote and mescaline are neither harmful to, nor misused by, human beings.

Speaking as a Native American, Vine Deloria, Professor of Law at the University of Colorado and author of *God is Red,* may overstate the case. Even so, there is substance in the statement he makes in the documentary film *The Peyote Road*:

> *The classification of peyote as a Schedule I narcotic is absurd. You can go to any city in the country and within three blocks downtown you can buy any drug you want. But the average American will spend weeks, or months even, locating a member of the Native American Church, let alone find one that has peyote on him. The situation is surrealistic.*

NOTES

1. Stephen J. Gould, "Taxonomy as Politics," *Dissent*, Winter 1990, 73–8.
2. E. F. Anderson, "The Biogeography, Ecology, and Taxonomy of *Lophophora* (Cactaceae)," *Brittonia*, 21:299–310.
3. E. F. Anderson, *Peyote: The Divine Cactus* (Tucson: The University of Arizona Press, 1980).
4. J. M. Adovasio and G. F. Fry, "Prehistoric Psychotropic Drug Use in Northeastern Mexico and Trans-Pecos Texas," *Economic Botany*, 30:94–96.
5. D. Sharon, "The San Pedro Cactus in Peruvian Folk Healing," in P. T. Furst, *Flesh of the Gods* (New York: Praeger, 1972).
6. S. W. Pelletier, "The Nature and Definition of an Alkaloid," in S. W. Pelletier (ed.), *Alkaloids: Chemical and Biological Perspectives*, Vol. 1 (New York: John Wiley and Sons, 1983).
7. G. R. Walter and E. K. Nowacki, *Alkaloid Biology and Metabolism in Plants* (New York: Plenum Press, 1978).
8. R. L. Bergman, "Navajo Peyote Use: Its Apparent Safety," *American Journal of Psychiatry*, 128 (1971), 695–9.
9. G. A. Feigen and G. A. Alles, "Physiological Concomitants of Mescaline Intoxication," *Journal of Clinical Experimental Psychopathology and Quarterly Review of Psychiatry and Neurology*,

16:167–78; P. Deniker, "Biological Changes in Man following Intravenous Administration of Mescaline," *Journal of Nervous and Mental Disease*, 125:427–31; A. M. Ludwig and J. Levine, "The Clinical Effects of Psychedelic Agents," *Clinical Medicine*, 73:21–4; and G. J. Kapadia and M. B. E. Fayez, "Peyote Constituents: Chemistry, Biogenesis, and Biological Effects," *Journal of Pharmaceutical Science*, 59:1699–1727.

10. B. L. Jacobs, "How Hallucinogenic Drugs Work," *American Scientist*, 75:386–92.

11. E. Jacobsen, "The Clinical Pharmacology of the Hallucinogens," *Clinical Pharmacology and Therapeutics*, 4:480–503.

12. J. S. Slotkin, *Menomini Peyotism* (Philadelphia: The American Philosophical Society, 1952), 569.

13. H. F. Hardman and C. O. Seevers, "Relationship of the Structure of Mescaline and Seven Analogs to Toxicity and Behavior in Five Species of Laboratory Animals," *Toxicology and Applied Pharmacology*, 25:299–309.

14. R. Underhill, "Peyote," in *Proceedings of the 30th International Congress of Americanists*, London 1952, 143–48.

15. P. C. Reynolds and E. J. Jindrich, "A Mescaline Associated Fatality," *Journal of Analytical Toxicology*, 9:183–4.

16. David L. Dorrance, M.D., Oscar Janiger, M.D., and Raymond L. Tepliz, M.D., "Effects of Peyote on Human Chromosomes," *Journal of the American Medical Association*, 1975, 234:299–302. Prefaced by Dr. Janiger's report in the documentary film, *The Peyote Road*.

17. M. H. Seevers, "Drug Addiction," in V. A. Drill (ed.), *Pharmacology in Medicine*, 2nd ed. (New York: McGraw-Hill, 1958).

18. Excerpted from testimony presented by Emery A. Johnson, M.D., to the House Subcommitte on Native American Affairs, March 16, 1993.

19. Robert L. Bergman, M.D., "Navajo Peyote Use: Its Apparent Safety," *American Journal of Psychiatry*, 128 (December, 1971): 695–9.

20. *Ibid.*, 699.
21. *Webster's Third New International Dictionary of the English Language*, unabridged, 1981, 1503.
22. R. E. Schultes and A. Hofmann, *Plants of the Gods* (New York: McGraw-Hill, 1979).
23. L. S. Goodman and A. Gilman, *The Pharmacological Basis of Therapeutics*, 4th ed. (New York: Macmillan, 1970).
24. Expert Committee on Drugs Liable to Produce Addiction, 1950, 6–7.
25. L. S. Goodman and A. Gilman, *op. cit.*
26. C. C. Pfeiffer and H. B. Murphree, "Introduction to Psychotropic Drugs and Hallucinogenic Drugs," in J. R. DiPalma (ed.), *Drill's Pharmacology in Medicine* (New York: McGraw-Hill, 1965), 321–36.
27. S. Szara, "The Hallucinogenic Drugs — Curse or Blessing?" in F. Braceland (ed.), *Drug Abuse: Medical and Criminal Aspects* (New York: MSS Information Corporation, 1972).
28. R. E. Schultes and A. Hofmann, *The Botany and Chemistry of Hallucinogens* (Springfield, Ill.: Charles C. Thomas, 1980), 15.

"Peyote Culture," watercolor, by Beatien Yazz. Courtesy of Oklahoma Indian Arts Gallery.

4

The Legal Tango: The Native American Church v. The United States of America

James Botsford and Walter B. Echo-Hawk

The Indian plays much the same role in our American society that the Jews played in Germany. Like the miner's canary, the Indian marks the shift from fresh air to poison gas in our political atmosphere; and our treatment of Indians, even more than our treatment of other minorities, marks the rise and fall of our democratic nation.

Felix Cohen, Father of Federal Indian Law

Because the religious use of the peyote cactus plant is unique to American Indians and little understood by outsiders, it has had a checkered (and at times chaotic) legal history under European rulers. When President Clinton signed into law the American Indian Religious Freedom Act Amendments of 1994, he brought to a close an epic struggle to protect an American religious practice that predates by millennia the whites' invasion of America.

The First Five Centuries

That struggle began on the day Christopher Columbus set foot in the New World. A few days later he wrote in his diary that the natives "would easily be made Christians because it seemed to me that they had no religion."[1] Missionaries soon learned otherwise. They went to great lengths to stamp out peyote use, ample testimony to their realization that it was powered by religious energies and that it was Christianity's

125

rival. In 1620 — the year the Pilgrims landed on Plymouth rock to escape persecution — the Catholic Church issued an edict against peyote and invoked the arm of the Inquisition to enforce it. Without success. Despite ninety prosecuted cases in the next two centuries, peyote rituals persisted, "especially among the tribes where it grew and farther north."[2]

The inability of the Catholic and other churches to suppress peyotism prompted the Department of the Interior, in 1883, to establish the Court of Indian Offenses. Its rules called for Indian agencies to prosecute users of intoxicants, rituals of medicine men, and "old heathen dances"; it also instructed agents to stop these practices on their own if the Court was not in session.[3] Five years later, on the Kiowa-Comanche Reservation, peyote was targeted explicitly. Federal Indian agents and missionaries posted an order stating that "all Indians on this Reservation are hereby forbidden to eat peyote or to drink any decoction or liquor distilled therefrom. Any Indian convicted of violating this order will be punished by cutting off his annuity goods and rations."[4]

These were administrative orders. The first statute law intending to criminalize the use of peyote was passed by the Oklahoma legislature in 1899. It stipulated that "it shall be unlawful for any person to introduce on any Indian reservation or to have in possession . . . any 'Mescal Bean,' or the product of any such drug."[5] To spot violators, Indian agents employed nonpeyotist Indians to spy on peyote meetings and files were kept on those who attended. There was a double irony here. First, the religion's sacrament was mistakenly identified as "mescal" (*Sophora secundiflora*) rather than peyote, and at least one court upheld an appeal from an Indian for that reason. The second irony was that while this law was in effect peyote could be purchased over the counter in drug stores; pharmaceutical firms such as Parke, Davis, and Company dispensed it regularly. Belief in its therapeutic virtues continued into the 1920s, with dosages prescribed in the *United States Dispensatory*.[6]

This reference to Oklahoma is not adventitious, for much of the NAC's early history centered there; in the late 1800s, from 35 to 90 percent of the members of the Oklahoma tribes belonged to the Church. When the territory was preparing for statehood early in this century, Indian agents prepared anti-peyote legislation, but sixteen peyotists lobbied against it so convincingly that it was defeated. Their move was supported by the Medical Committee of the 1908 Constitutional Convention, one of whose members told the chiefs: "This is your religion like my white church. Keep it for your younger children so that they too will preserve it for future generations."[7]

Even without legal backing, however, harassment continued. When in 1909 the Bureau of Indian Affairs appointed a special officer to deal with Oklahoma's "peyote problem," he first tried to get its courts to rule that peyote use was included in the current prohibition laws. Failing in that attempt, he raided peyote meetings at will, destroying all the buttons he could get his hands on. He even tried to persuade pharmacists to stop stocking the substance, but they argued that even if it was questionable for Indians, it did whites no harm.[8]

Oklahoma was not alone in such harassments. In 1911 a federal Indian agent rounded up South Dakota peyotists and jailed them with no legal authority whatsoever. In 1913, 1916, and 1917 motions were introduced in Congress to amend the

Indian Prohibition Act by including the words "and peyote" after "intoxicating liquors," but none of them advanced beyond committee. This, however, did not prevent agents from using the Act as a pretext for arresting peyotists.

With this failure to enact a federal law against peyotism, Utah, Nevada, and Colorado took matters into their own hands and passed laws criminalizing it in their states. Kansas, Arizona, Montana, North Dakota, and South Dakota followed suit in 1923; Iowa in 1925; New Mexico and Wyoming in 1929; and Idaho in 1933. During these years the federal government contented itself with authorizing (until 1934) an annual line item of $25,000 for the suppression of Indian peyote use, and in 1919 the Bureau of Indian Affairs published a strongly worded anti-peyote pamphlet, *Peyote*, which was widely distributed.

The 1934 appointment of John Collier as Commissioner for Indian Affairs brought a marked change of attitude. The hostile pamphlet *Peyote* was withdrawn and replaced with a Bureau Circular which said that "no interference with Indian religious life or ceremonial expression will hereafter be tolerated." This diminished stigma and harassment, though prosecutions continued sporadically.[9]

The last Congressional attempt to legislate against peyote occurred in 1963, but by this time anthropologists were siding with the Indians and the bill died in committee. Two years later Congress passed the Drug Abuse Control Amendments with express intent to protect Indian ceremonial use of peyote, and when in the following year the Administration moved peyote into the category of Schedule I controlled substances, the Drug Enforcement Administration expressly stipulated that "this does not apply to the non-drug use of peyote in bona fide religious ceremonies of the Native American Church" (21 C.F.R. Section 1307.31). Non-Indian peyote-using "churches" that have sprung up in recent years have argued that this exemption discriminates against them, but in 1991 the Fifth Circuit Court of Appeals ruled that the U.S. government's trust relationship with tribal Native Americans places them in a special category that makes their exemption in order.

> We hold that the federal NAC exemption allowing tribal Native Americans to continue their centuries-old tradition of peyote use is rationally related to the legitimate governmental objective of preserving Native American culture. [Non-Indians] are not similarly situated [with respect to] cultural preservation.[10]

That decision was relatively late. In these confusing years, the 1964 case of *People v. Woody, et. al.* stands out as something of a landmark and deserves special attention.

In the spring of 1962 an elder of the Otoe-Missouri Indian Tribe, Truman Dailey, who as of this writing is ninety-six-years-old (see his testimonial on pages 38–39, 57–58), conducted a Peyote Meeting for Navajo railroad workers in a desert hogan near Needles, California. State police raided the meeting and arrested three of the Navajo participants: Jack Woody, Dan Nex, and Leon Anderson. They were jailed and charged with illegal use of peyote. Frank Takes Gun, who was President of the Native American Church of North America at the time, persuaded the ACLU to defend the Indians and arranged for expert witnesses that included the respected anthropologist, Omer Stewart. At the trial the three Indians pleaded not guilty, contending that their possession of peyote was an integral part of their religious faith, and hence that the California law that outlawed the plant's consumption infringed on their religious freedom and violated the First Amendment of the United States Constitution.

Following a widely publicized trial in San Bernardino, the County Court found the defendants guilty, stating that "the Native American Church must forsake its peyote rituals in deference to the unqualified legislative command of prohibition." The convictions were upheld by the Court of Appeals, but the Supreme Court of California reversed them and the Indians were freed. In this landmark decision, the Court ruled that, given the fact that peyote religious practices harmed no one, the state had no compelling reason to stop it, and doing so violated the First Amendment. In the course of the trial the State claimed that peyote use was harmful to Indians and that an Indian religious exemption would adversely impact State enforcement of its drug laws. The Court reviewed these claims and rejected them as unproven speculation. "The State's showing of a 'compelling state interest' cannot lie in untested assertions," it decreed, adding:

> [We] have weighed the competing values represented in this case on the symbolic scale of constitutionality. On the one side, we have placed the weight of freedom of religion as protected by the First Amendment; on the other, the weight of the state's "compelling interest." Since the use of peyote incorporates the essence of the religious expression, the first weight is heavy. Yet the use of peyote presents only slight danger to the state and to the enforcement of its laws, so the second weight is relatively light. The scale tips in favor of the constitutional protection.

The Court went on to indicate the benefits for all Americans that derived from its determination to keep the First Amendment in solid place.

> We know that some will urge that it is more important to subserve the rigorous enforcement of the narcotic laws than to carve out of them an exception for a few believers in a strange faith. They will say that the exception may produce problems of enforcement and that the dictate of the state must overcome the beliefs of a minority of Indians. But the problems of enforcement here do not inherently differ from those of other situations which call for the detection of fraud. On the other hand, the right to free exercise of religious expression embodies a precious heritage of our history. In a mass society, which presses at every point toward conformity, the protection of a self-expression, however unique, of the individual and the group becomes ever more important. The varying currents of the subcultures that flow into the mainstream of our national life give it depth and beauty. We preserve a greater value than an ancient tradition when we protect the rights of the Indians who honestly practiced an old religion in using peyote one night at a meeting in a desert hogan near Needles, California.[11]

In reaffirming the high ideals that the Founding Fathers sought to enshrine in the Bill of Rights, the *Woody* decision stands as a classic example of American justice at its best. In 1973 it was reaffirmed in appeals from the *State of Arizona v. Whittingham* decision. Police had raided a hogan in Parks, Arizona, where a Native American Church prayer meeting was being held to bless a recent marriage, and about forty Indians and non-Indians were arrested. Of these, two were convicted, but they appealed and their convictions were overturned. In freeing them, the appellate court reviewed the State's claims that it needed to protect Indians against the "ill effects" of peyote and found it wanting. The State had not, it said, proved ill effects to public health, safety, or morals sufficient to establish a compelling interest in restricting the religious practice of Native American Church members.

> The uncontroverted evidence on the record is that peyote is not a narcotic substance and is not habit forming. The fact that the use of peyote will not result in addiction is crucial because the State would have a great interest in protecting its citizens from drug abuse. Had the addictive qualities of peyote been proven, the State's interest would be stronger because of the possible burden upon our resources that an addict can become if the State is forced to assume the maintenance of this individual. Furthermore, the State failed to prove that the quantities of peyote used in the sacraments of the Native American Church are sufficiently harmful to the health and welfare of the participants so as to permit a legitimate intrusion under the State's police power.

As in Woody, the Arizona court emphasized the bona fide and longstanding religious tradition of the Native American Church:

> We must emphasize that the record, and the trial court's findings, made several determinations in which peyotism was found to be an established religion of many centuries' history. Suffice it to say, therefore, that peyotism is not a twentieth century cult nor a fad subject to extinction at a whim. Most of the members who testified at trial, e.g., were active participants in the Native American Church and had been for years; in fact, in many instances, for

decades. The religion is established with a following of several hundred thousand believers.[12]

When in 1977 the spotlight moved from Arizona to Oklahoma, its Court of Criminal Appeals again vindicated the Indians. When stopped for a traffic offense, an Otoe Indian was found to have peyote on his person and was convicted for possessing it in violation of Oklahoma's controlled substance law. On appeal, the Court held that

> *the State did not present evidence which would sustain a finding of a state interest in regulation compelling enough to prohibit the exercise of the religious practice of peyotism by the Native American Church and its members. From the record before us it is apparent that the Native American Church is recognized by the State of Oklahoma and has a statewide organization of local chapters. It is, therefore, our opinion that in a prosecution for possession of peyote under the provisions of the Uniform Controlled Dangerous Substances Act it is a defense to show that the peyote was being used in connection with a bona fide practice of the Native American Church and that it was used or possessed in a manner not dangerous to the public health, safety or morals.*[13]

Through these three cases, California, Arizona, and Oklahoma confirmed the right of the Native American Church to First Amendment protection. Other states, however, behaved differently. In *State of Oregon v. Soto*, 1975, for example, the Court refused to allow the defendant to enter evidence of his belief that peyote is an integral part of the religious ceremonies of the Native American Church and that he possessed it for religious purposes alone. Nor was it clear if the federal government protected the NAC, for its legitimization of Indian peyotism was only an administrative regulation.

This muddled state of affairs changed abruptly when the United States Supreme Court delivered, on April 17, 1990, what some consider the most infamous ruling in its history. All but reversing the principles relating to religion which have made the United States unique, *Employment Division of Oregon v. Smith*[14] stands as a blot on the Supreme Court's character and needs to be considered in detail.

1990–1993: The Smith Decision and Its Aftermath

The story of the *Smith* decision revolves around Alfred Leo Smith, a member of the Klamath Nation in Oregon, whose childhood was spent on a reservation and in boarding schools. As a young adult he suffered from alcoholism, but by the age of thirty-six had recovered through Alcoholics Anonymous. Sweat lodge experiences brought him in touch with his native spirituality which eventually guided him to the Native American Church (excerpts from his own personal accounts appear on pages 51–52 and 68 of this book). Deciding that he wanted to devote the remainder of his life to countering the devastation that alcohol was wreaking on Indian people, he developed Native American programs for alcohol and drug treatment. His last job in that field was in Roseburg, Oregon, where he was hired to help develop services for Native clientele. In 1984, its director learned that Smith and one of his co-workers attended the Native American Church. The co-worker, a non-Indian, was fired on the spot, and Smith was fired when he refused to stop attending Church meetings.

Neither of the men sought job reinstatement, but they did

ask for the unemployment compensation that was denied them. That led to six years of litigation in which the Oregon employment appeals board ruled that they were *not* entitled to the benefits; the Oregon Court of Appeals said they *were* entitled to them, and the Oregon State Supreme Court agreed with that ruling when the state's Attorney General challenged it. Still dissatisfied with the vindication of Native American Church members, the Oregon Attorney General referred the case to the United States Supreme Court which, on April 17, 1990, delivered the decision which overturned the ruling of Oregon's highest court.

We have seen that in the long, checkered history of this most regulated religion in America it was often the courts which, backed by the First Amendment's humane provisions, upheld the Indians' rights to religious freedom. *Woody, Whittingham,* and *Whitehorn* show the American legal system at its potential best, acting as a watchdog to keep insensitive majorities from pushing helpless people around. Legislatures in this century have been less enlightened; it was the courts that — in some of the most moving decisions in the history of American jurisprudence — saved the day. It is ironic, therefore, that it was the highest court of the land that reversed this picture as the century entered its closing decade. In *Smith,* the Supreme Court stripped the Native American Church of Constitutional protection altogether. Over the decades, state courts had moved slowly but steadily toward singling out the NAC for protection. The Supreme Court singled it out to deny it protection.

It did so by arguing that, in order to interfere with Native American religious rights, Oregon did not have to show that there was a compelling reason to do so. Through hundreds of federal and state cases relating to American religious freedom in the last two hundred years, the phrase "compelling state interest" had emerged as the test; unless the state could prove that there was a compelling need for it to intervene, it was not entitled to do so. To support its retreat from this well entrenched legal precedent, Justice Scalia argued that America's religious diversity had become a "luxury" that a pluralistic society could no longer "afford," and that, since this was the case, the "compelling state interest" test had to be withdrawn.[15] In addition, the Court removed from First Amendment protection an entire body of law: criminal law. This, in effect, rewrote the First Amendment to read, "Congress shall make no laws except criminal laws that prohibit the free exercise of religion." Finally, the Court suggested that the First Amendment does not protect the free exercise of religion unless some other First Amendment right, such as speech or association, is involved. This, of course, makes religious freedom irrelevant, for those other rights are independently protected.

The far-reaching implications of *Smith* sent shockwaves through the American religious community as a whole, for the principles that it explicitly directed at a powerless minority religion could be used against any religion should occasion arise. The day after the decision was delivered witnessed the formation of the largest religious coalition in American history to ask the Court to reconsider its ruling, but without avail. The Supreme Court justices that dissented in *Smith* were also appalled. Justice Blackmun wrote:

*I do not believe the Founders thought their dearly bought freedom
from religious persecution a "luxury," but an essential element of
liberty — and they could not have thought religious intolerance
"unavoidable," for they drafted the Religion Clauses precisely in
order to avoid that intolerance.*[16]

Even Justice O'Connor, who concurred with the decision's
verdict on peyote, took strong exception to the way the Court
had reasoned on the matter. "In my view," she wrote in a
separate opinion, "today's ruling dramatically departs from
well established First Amendment jurisprudence, appears un-
necessary to resolve the question presented, and is incompati-
ble with our Nation's commitment to individual religious
liberty." Even the majority opinion recognized that its decision
would "place at a relative disadvantage those religious practices that are not widely engaged in," but it threw the Native
American Church a sop by advising that its members turn to
legislatures to win back the rights the Court had stripped them
of. Justice O'Connor pointed out the hollowness of this conde-
scending gesture by quoting Justice Jackson in an earlier case:

*The very purpose of the Bill of Rights was to withdraw certain sub-
jects from the vicissitudes of political controversy, to place them
beyond the reach of majorities and officials and to establish them
as legal principles to be applied by the courts. One's right to life,
liberty, and property, to free speech, a free press, freedom of worship and assembly, and other fundamental rights may not be sub-
mitted to vote; they depend on the outcome of no election.*[17]

Speaking for herself, Justice O'Connor added:

The First Amendment was enacted precisely to protect the rights

*of those whose religious practices are not shared by the majority
and may be viewed with hostility. The history of our free exercise
doctrine amply demonstrates the harsh impact majoritarian rule
has had upon unpopular or emerging religious groups such as the
Jehovah's Witnesses and the Amish.*[18]

The *Smith* decision was devastating to the Native American
Church. For four and a half years that decision forced it
underground in a way reminiscent of the catacombs. Arrests
were on the minds of its members as they lived like criminals
fearing the knock on the door. It was as if Columbus had been
right: Indians had no religion — none worth protecting by
law. A new addition to the Supreme Court, Justice Souter,
urged that *Smith* be re-examined,[19] but his recommendation
fell on deaf ears.

As has been noted, however, the intolerable implications of
the decision aroused widespread concern, and when the Court
refused to reconsider its decision, the major religious denominations in the country formed the Religious Freedom Restoration Act Coalition to win back by law the religious rights that
the Supreme Court had stripped from the First Amendment. A
Native American leader who was rousing and consolidating action on the Indian front, Reuben Snake, tried to get the Coalition to mention Indian rights explicitly in the bill it hoped to
get through Congress, for it was Indians who had taken the di-
rect hit in *Smith*. Leaders of the Coalition rejected his plea,
however, saying that its constituency was so diverse in its per-
suasions that reinstatement of the "compelling state interest"
test was the only thing they could agree on; if a single sentence
were added to that, the Coalition would collapse. The Coali-

tion did succeed in that single object, however. On June 30, 1993, Congress passed the Religious Freedom Restoration Act, and the compelling interest test was reinstated.

This was progress, but as Reuben Snake had pointed out to the Coalition, it did not resolve the Native American Church's dilemma. There were two things wrong with the way the Religious Freedom Restoration Act left things.

First, though the "compelling state interest" clause was back in place, the door remained open for judges to conclude that compelling reasons for outlawing peyote exist. Actually, Justice O'Connor's opinion had taken exactly this route. As we have seen, she concurred with the majority against the Native American Church, but differed from the others on her side by arguing that their ruling went too far. It needn't have scuttled the "compelling state interest" test. It would have been enough to keep it in place and rule that the Native American Church flunked it.

The second reason why further action was needed was that many states still outlawed peyote. As the Religious Freedom Restoration Act spoke only in general terms, judges could conclude that in the case of peyote they had no choice but to abide by the laws of their states.

After 1993

Logically this is where, arguably, the finest hour in Native American history begins, though chronologically it began on the day the *Smith* decision was delivered. Reuben Snake, one of the greatest Native American leaders of this century, realized immediately that if *Smith* were allowed to stand it could be the death knell of a crucial dimension of Native American life, undermining family and cultural cohesiveness through destroying a spiritual tradition that extended back thousands of years. With the endorsement of elected Church leaders, he created the strongest coalition in Native American Church history, the Native American Religious Freedom Project, to deal directly with Washington. At the outset his project appeared impossible: overturn the highest court of the land without a dime in his coffers! When he was asked how he proposed to accomplish the task he replied, "With a frequent flyer coupon and a prayer."

The working group that Snake put together was more diverse than the first Coalition. Many of the religious groups in the initial Coalition continued their interest and joined with Indian tribes, Native rights organizations, and movie stars to form a broadly based movement. Public sentiment and the press were mostly on its side. A documentary film, *The Peyote Road* (see page 10), was produced to aid the effort; it portrayed the NAC with a clarity that the outside world had not hitherto seen. Dozens of conferences and symposia were convened to spread awareness of the problem. Summit level meetings among tribal leaders planned strategy, and congressmen were induced to hold hearings on the need for added legislation. Elected leaders and elders of the NAC organizations across the country started drafting a bill to present to Congress, one they hoped would insure the religious liberties of Native Americans forever.

Senator Daniel K. Inouye, Chairman of the Senate Committee on Indian Affairs, provided the congressional leadership necessary to advance this issue by conducting field hearings throughout Indian country and sponsoring the first version of the new, proposed bill. These were followed by House oversight hearings in 1993, and on April 14, 1994, Bill Richardson of New Mexico, Chairman of the Subcommittee on Native American Affairs of the Natural Resources Committee, introduced H.R. 4230 in the House of Representatives. Specifically intended to create a uniform national law that would protect Indian religious use of peyote, it was supported by NAC leaders. A hearing on the bill was held by the Subcommittee on June 10, which advanced it on July 22. The Drug Enforcement Administration continued its long history of cooperation with the NAC by providing supportive testimony; in this it was joined by the Department of Justice. On July 27, 1994, the bill, with amendments, was passed along by the Committee on Natural Resources. The House of Representatives passed it by unanimous voice vote on August 8, 1994.

When the bill reached the Senate, it was placed on the Unanimous Consent Calendar by Senators Inouye and McCain. A number of anonymous Republican holds were placed on the bill, and it was referred to the Senate Committee on Indian Affairs. After negotiations with the relevant Republican Senators, the holds were lifted. This paved the way for unanimous consent for discharging the bill from Committee. It was passed on September 27, 1994. President Clinton signed it into law on October 6, 1994, and the centuries-long era of persecution and oppression of Native American peyotism was ended.

When asked how his humble church could ever hope to educate Americans enough to overcome the devastation of *Smith*, Reuben Snake had smiled and said, "We'll find good friends along the way." And so it was.

NOTES

1. Quoted in Kirkpatrick Sale, *The Conquest of Paradise* (New York: Alfred A. Knopf, 1990), 96–7.
2. Omer C. Stewart, *Peyote Religion: A History* (Norman: University of Oklahoma Press, 1987), 26.
3. *Ibid.*, 130.
4. Christopher Vecsey (ed.), *Handbook of American Indian Religious Freedom* (New York: Crossroad Publishing Company, 1991), 44–5.
5. *Ibid.*, 131.
6. Omer C. Stewart, *Peyote Religion*, 131.
7. *Ibid.*, 136.
8. *Ibid.*, 138–9.
9. *Ibid.*, 237–8.
10. *Peyote Way Church of God v. Thornburgh*, 922 F.2d 1210 (5th Cir., 1991).
11. *People v. Woody, et al.* 394 P.2d 813 (Ca. Sup. Ct., 1964).
12. *State of Arizona v. Whittingham*, 504 P. 2d 950 (Az. Ct. Appeals; 1973).
13. *Whitehorn v. State of Oklahoma*, 561 P.2d 142 (Or. App., 1975).
14. *Employment Division of Oregon v. Smith*, 494 U.S. 872 (1990).
15. *Ibid.*, at 892 and 888–93.
16. *Ibid.*, at 909.
17. *Ibid.*, at 902.
18. *Ibid.*
19. In *Church of Lukumi v. Hialeah*, 1993.

5

Public Law 103-344
The American Indian Religious
Freedom Act Amendments of 1994

The determination of Native Americans to win back the freedoms the Supreme Court took from them can be compared to the three stages of a rocket's take-off.

Stage One: Native Americans joined with other churches to secure the passage of the American Indian Religious Freedom Act Amendments of 1994, even though their own rights were not guaranteed by that Act.

Stage Two: The silence of that Act on their distinctive rights led leaders of the Native American Church to mount their own Native American Religious Freedom Project whose efforts culminated in the passage (on October 6, 1994) of the law that forms the text of this chapter.

Stage Three is ongoing. Prohibition of the sacramental use of peyote is not the only way the religious freedoms of Native American peoples have been curtailed. Other infringements relate to: (1) the preservation of their sacred sites; (2) the right of imprisoned Indians to religious ministrations comparable to those that other inmates receive (sweat lodges to parallel Holy Communion, for example); and (3) their right to have access to animal parts that are important for their religious practices — such as eagle feathers, to cite a single instance. To work for these other rights as well as those pertaining to peyote, the Native American Religious Freedom Project (which focused on the peyote issue) broadened into the American Indian Religious Freedom Coalition. Its work continues.

On signing the 1993 Religious Freedom Restoration Act in a ceremony in the Rose Garden, President Clinton said, "The signing of [today's] legislation by the President assumes a majestic quality because we affirm the historical role people of faith have played in our country, and the constitutional protections those who profess and express their faith have historically enjoyed." When he went on to add that those protections "will not be complete until traditional Native American religious practices have received the protection they deserve," his words could have been read as a call for the Act the Native Americans put together for him to sign a year later.

That Act is rendered here in two versions. The first is a paraphrase of the law which, stripped of its legalese, makes its provisions readily accessible to the general reader. That paraphrase is followed by the Law proper, reprinted from the *Congressional Record*.

Public Law 103–344, Paraphrased

The Congress finds and declares that for many Indian people the traditional ceremonial use of the peyote cactus as a religious sacrament has for centuries been integral to a way of life, and significant in perpetuating Indian tribes and cultures.

Since 1965 this ceremonial use of peyote by Indians has been protected by federal regulation. In addition, at least 28 States have enacted laws which are similar to, or are in conformance with, the federal regulation which protects the ceremonial use of peyote by Indian religious practitioners. However, 22 states have not done so, and this lack of uniformity has created hardship for Indian people who participate in such religious ceremonies.

The Supreme Court of the United States, in the case of *Employment Division of Oregon v. Smith*, held that the First Amendment does not protect Indian practitioners who use peyote in Indian religious ceremonies, and also created uncertainty as to whether this religious practice would be protected under the compelling-state-interest standard. This lack of adequate and clear legal protection for the religious use of peyote by Indians may serve to stigmatize and marginalize Indian tribes and cultures, and increase the risk that they will be exposed to discriminatory treatment.

Notwithstanding any other provision of law, the use, possession, or transportation of peyote by an Indian for bona fide traditional ceremonial purposes in connection with the practice of a traditional Indian religion, is lawful and shall not be prohibited by the United States or any State. No Indian shall be penalized or discriminated against for such use, possession, or transportation, or denied otherwise applicable benefits under public assistance programs.

This law does not prohibit reasonable regulation and registration by the Drug Enforcement Administration of persons who cultivate, harvest, or distribute peyote, provided such codes are consistent with the purposes of this Act.

Nothing in this law prohibits any federal department or agency from promulgating regulations that reasonably limit the use or ingestion of peyote by its employees prior to or during the performance of their official duties if these employees are involved in safety-sensitive positions (such as law-enforcement officers or those directly involved in public transportation), and if their job performance may be adversely affected by such use or ingestion. However, such regulations shall be adopted only after consultation with representatives of traditional Indian religions for which the sacramental use of peyote is integral to their practices. Henceforth, any regulation that is promulgated must conform to the balancing test set forth in section 3 of the 1993 Religious Freedom Restoration Act.

This Act does not require prison authorities to permit, nor prohibit prison authorities from permitting, access to peyote by Indians while incarcerated within federal or state prison facilities.

Subject to the provisions of the Religious Freedom Restoration Act, the present Act does not prohibit states from enacting or enforcing reasonable traffic-safety laws or regulations.

Subject to the provisions of the Religious Freedom Restoration Act, the present Act does not prohibit the Secretary of Defense from promulgating regulations establishing reasonable limitations on the use, possession, transportation, or distribution of peyote to promote military readiness, safety, or compliance with international law or the laws of other countries. Such regulations shall be adopted only after consultation with representatives of traditional Indian religions for which the sacramental use of peyote is integral to their practice.

For purposes of this Act, the term "Indian" means a member of an Indian tribe. The term "Indian tribe" means any tribe, band, nation, pueblo, or other organized group or community of Indians, including any Alaska Native village which is recognized as eligible for the special programs and services provided by the United States to Indians because of their status as Indians.

The term "Indian religion" means any religion which is practiced by Indians, the origins and beliefs of which are as a traditional Indian culture or community understands them.

The term "State" means any State of the United States, and any political subdivision thereof.

Nothing in this Act shall be construed as abrogating, diminishing, or otherwise affecting the inherent rights of any Indian tribe; the inherent right of Indians to practice their religions; and the right of Indians to practice their religions under any federal or state law.

Public Law 103–344

In its actual wording, as it appears in the Congressional Record, the Law reads as follows:

PUBLIC LAW 103–344—OCT. 6, 1994

108 STAT. 3125

Public Law 103–344
103d Congress

An Act

To amend the American Indian Religious Freedom Act to provide for the traditional use of peyote by Indians for religious purposes, and for other purposes.

Be it enacted by the Senate and House of Representatives of the United States of America in Congress assembled,

SECTION 1. SHORT TITLE.

This Act may be cited as the "American Indian Religious Freedom Act Amendments of 1994."

SEC. 2.   TRADITIONAL INDIAN RELIGIOUS USE OF THE PEYOTE SACRAMENT.

The Act of August 11, 1978 (42 U.S.C. 1996), commonly referred to as the "American Indian Religious Freedom Act," is amended by adding at the end thereof the following new section:

"SEC. 3 (a) The Congress finds and declares that—

"(1) for many Indian people, the traditional ceremonial use of the peyote cactus as a religious sacrament has for centuries been integral to a way of life, and significant in perpetuating Indian tribes and cultures;

"(2) since 1965, this ceremonial use of peyote by Indians has been protected by Federal regulation;

"(3) while at least 28 States have enacted laws which are similar to, or are in conformance with, the Federal regulation which protects the ceremonial use of peyote by Indian religious practitioners, 22 States have not done so, and this lack of uniformity has created hardship for Indian people who participate in such religious ceremonies;

"(4) the Supreme Court of the United States, in the case of Employment Division v. Smith, 494 U.S. 872 (1990), held that the First Amendment does not protect Indian practitioners who use peyote in Indian religious ceremonies, and also raised uncertainty whether this religious practice would be protected under the compelling State interest standard; and

"(5) the lack of adequate and clear legal protection for the religious use of peyote by Indians may serve to stigmatize and marginalize Indian tribes and cultures, and increase the risk that they will be exposed to discriminatory treatment.

"(b)(1) Notwithstanding any other provision of law, the use, possession, or transportation of peyote by an Indian for bona fide traditional ceremonial purposes in connection with the practice of a traditional Indian religion is lawful, and shall not be prohibited by the United States, or any State. No Indian shall be penalized or discriminated against on the basis of such use, possession or transportation, including, but not limited to, denial of otherwise applicable benefits under public assistance programs.

"(2) This section does not prohibit such reasonable regulation and registration by the Drug Enforcement Administration of those persons who cultivate, harvest, or distribute peyote as may be consistent with the purposes of this Act.

"(3) This section does not prohibit application of the provisions of section 481.111(a) of Vernon's Texas Health and Safety Code Annotated, in effect on the date of enactment of this section, insofar as those provisions pertain to the cultivation, harvest, and distribution of peyote.

"(4) Nothing in this section shall prohibit any Federal department or agency, in carrying out its statutory responsibilities and functions, from promulgating regulations establishing reasonable limitations on the use or ingestion of peyote prior to or during the performance of duties by sworn law enforcement officers or personnel directly involved in public transportation or any other safety-sensitive positions where the performance of such duties may be adversely affected by such use or ingestion. Such regulations shall be adopted only after consultation with representatives of traditional Indian religions for which the sacramental use of peyote is integral to their practice. Any regulation promulgated pursuant to this section shall be subject to the balancing test set forth in section 3 of the Religious Freedom Restoration Act (Public Law 103–141; 42 U.S.C. 2000bb–1).

"(5) This section shall not be construed as requiring prison authorities to permit, nor shall it be construed to prohibit prison authorities from permitting, access to peyote by Indians while incarcerated within Federal or State prison facilities.

"(6) Subject to the provisions of the Religious Freedom Restoration Act (Public Law 103–141; 42 U.S.C. 2000bb–1), this section shall not be construed to prohibit States from enacting or enforcing reasonable traffic safety laws or regulations.

"(7) Subject to the provisions of the Religious Freedom Restoration Act (Public Law 103–141; 42 U.S.C. 2000bb–1), this section does not prohibit the Secretary of Defense from promulgating regulations establishing reasonable limitations on the use, possession, transportation, or distribution of peyote to promote military readiness, safety, or compliance with international law or laws of other countries. Such regulations shall be adopted only after consultation with representatives of traditional Indian religions for which the sacramental use of peyote is integral to their practice.

"(c) For purposes of this section—

"(1) the term 'Indian' means a member of an Indian tribe;

"(2) the term 'Indian tribe' means any tribe, band, nation, pueblo, or other organized group or community of Indians, including any Alaska Native village (as defined in, or established pursuant to, the Alaska Native Claims Settlement Act (43 U.S.C. 1601 et seq.)), which is recognized as eligible for the special programs and services provided by the United States to Indians because of their status as Indians;

"(3) the term 'Indian religion' means any religion—

"(A) which is practiced by Indians, and

"(B) the origin and interpretation of which is from within a traditional Indian culture or community; and

"(4) the term 'State' means any State of the United States, and any political subdivision thereof.

"(d) Nothing in this section shall be construed as abrogating, diminishing, or otherwise affecting—

"(1) the inherent rights of any Indian tribe;

"(2) the rights, express or implicit, of any Indian tribe which exist under treaties, Executive orders, and laws of the United States;

"(3) the inherent right of Indians to practice their religions; and

"(4) the right of Indians to practice their religions under any Federal or State law."

Approved October 6, 1994

LEGISLATIVE HISTORY—H.R. 4230:

HOUSE REPORTS: No. 103–675 (Comm. on Natural Resources).

CONGRESSIONAL RECORD, Vol. 140 (1994): Aug. 8, considered and passed House; Sept. 26, considered and passed Senate.

The American Indian Religious Freedom Act Amendments of 1994 was ruled unconstitutional by the U.S. Supreme Court on June 25, 1997, on the grounds that it "exceeds Congress's power."

Morning Water, *oil painting by Hayna Brown.*

Epilogue

The Death of a Roadman

The Family of Reuben Snake

It is unusual for a book to include an account of the death of one
of its editors. But because the Native American Church infused
Reuben Snake's life (1920–1993) to the point of being incarnat-
ed in that life, the way he managed his death provides an addi-
tional window (supplementing the one his Introduction provides)
onto what that Church can mean to its members.

The following account has been distilled from taped reports
by two of his brothers, Norman and John Snake, and his son
Darren Snake. —Editor

Shortly before his death, Reuben reported two important dreams. In the first, he saw himself standing next
to a river in a beautiful wooded area. His oldest brother, Peter John, appeared before him carrying a peace pipe. He
proposed that they smoke the pipe together, but Reuben woke
up before they did so. He awoke abruptly, regretful that they
had not had that smoke together.

Two weeks before he died, Reuben completed that first
dream. Again his brother brought him the peace pipe, but this
time they smoked it. Then, still in the dream, they began to
walk. They came to a large Indian village where a meeting was
in session. In the course of the meeting, Reuben glimpsed
something that glittered like gold. It was moving, and it
sparkled so brightly that it captured his attention. He walked
toward it and found Sterling Snake, his other older brother,

holding a golden eagle feather with which he fanned Reuben, brushing away his impurities.

That second dream occurred in the intensive care unit of the Sioux City hospital, and as Reuben awoke he found that he was praying, "God, let me make it home one more time. I want to take that Peyote Medicine. I want to sit in the tepee. I want to hear that drumming, hear that singing, and one more time I want to experience all those wonderful things we have in the Native American Church."

Reuben did return home, and his prayer for a final farewell meeting was answered. His family spoke of it as a thank-you (ta tanka) meeting for Reuben's life.

Word of the meeting got around, and relatives began to converge on the Winnebago reservation in Nebraska from considerable distances. The good feelings that attend such gatherings were present in abundance. Bonds re-formed among aunts, uncles, and cousins who had not seen one another for years. Endless reminiscences. People regrouping, moving from place to place. Coffee always available; things to eat. Sharing news of what was happening in Black River Falls, or the speaker's home town wherever it might be. A lot of teasing, "and do we Indians ever know how to tease!" The joy of being together, with Reuben (in his wheelchair and breathing from his oxygen tank) the focus of attention and the happiest in the crowd — happy that all these people had come together to bid him farewell.

In the afternoon the tepee was raised. With all the men pitching in, it seemed to go up in no time at all. As evening approached, the women had supper waiting. All eyes were on Reuben. He was eating, talking with those who were near him, and enjoying himself thoroughly.

After supper people from other tribes began to arrive for the meeting. They greeted Reuben and he expressed his obvious pleasure that they had made their journeys for the occasion. As many as could crowded into the tepee; the remainder surrounded it outdoors where they remained throughout the night.

Reuben's son Darren, who with his brothers had sponsored the meeting, served as Roadman. He noted the purpose of the meeting — to lift up praise and gratitude for his father's life — and then offered a prayer of unity and thanksgiving. The singing began and the Medicine was circulated as the Fireman kept adding wood to the fire and kept smoothing its coals into a beautiful bed. A bucket of water was passed, and people were invited to tell Reuben what he had meant to their lives.

Throughout the night Reuben, seated in his wheelchair, passed up the staff when it came by him and did not sing. On its last round, however, as dawn was breaking, he took his turn and rose to the occasion. He seized the staff and in his native tongue sang the songs of the Church with all of the energy and fervor that had become his signature in his later years, shaking his rattle in time with the rapid beat of the drummer on his left.

When Reuben's singing stopped, Darren asked his father to talk. Reuben began by turning the thank-you meeting for him into his thank-you meeting for his relatives and friends who had gathered. He then turned to Darren and bequeathed to him the ceremonial artifacts that had supported his (Reuben's) life. These included the prayer staff that had come down to him through Michael White Snake from Thomas Earth, the man who had carved it. They also included Chief Peyote (a blessed Peyote button), an eaglebone whistle, a wooden flute, an altar cloth and the eagle feather which is placed on top of it, an eagletail fan, a bundle of sage, and a drum. To his wife he bequeathed the pail in which she had so often carried consecrated water, and the set of bowls in which morning food is offered before it is consumed by the congregation.

In transmitting the objects to his wife and son he said, "These sacred objects will take care of you. They will provide a way and a home for you. If anyone needs your prayers, pray for them." Darren later reported that through these words, his father was relinquishing the objects that had sustained his life. He would not live long without them.

Then, turning to all who were gathered in the tepee, and by extension those who ringed it outdoors, Reuben spoke to his family at large. Beginning with his grandchildren, he told them with tears in his eyes how much he loved them, and he admonished them to treasure their Hochunk heritage. "If you put God first in your life you won't get lost. You won't need to use drugs, alcohol, or join gangs."

To everyone, he said that he was trying to find words to convey to them how much God had blessed him and all of them. He then turned to the Spirit directly, and addressed it in words that impressed his brother Norman so much that he wrote them down when the meeting was over.

The Spirit's here. You can almost see it, but you can't touch it. Reach out and it is there for the taking. So do that. Reach out. Lay hold of it and apply it to your lives. Use it, forever and forever. For if you just reach out, it will be there. It has been with us — not just with me but with us all — all this time, but because it's invisible we didn't realize it. But it was with us all the while.

Many spoke afterwards of those words as the climactic moment of the night for them. In that setting, coming from Reuben's mouth as his death was imminent, what he said seemed indubitable.

Though he had spent the night in his wheelchair, when the meeting concluded Reuben was able to leave the tepee on his own legs after first circumambulating the sacred fire for the last time.

At breakfast everyone was in the best of spirits. Reuben sang one of his favorite Morning Songs, a song of praise. He ate some Medicine, drank holy water, and ate the morning meal that he had requested in advance: Indian soup and fry bread. "What a beautiful day!" someone observed; and when it was pointed out that the name of the woman who had made that observation was Blue Sky, everyone laughed.

As the day unfolded, the men turned to dismantling the tepee, the women to dishes and general cleanup. Catnaps were taken, and the reminiscing continued.

In afternoon Reuben's mood began to change. It became more serious while in ways more childlike. At one point he curled up on the couch in the fetal position, remarking that we come into this world as children and exit it as children. He talked soberly to his brothers about the pain he had experienced when he returned from military service in Germany and found that they had been placed in foster homes. By later reports from the survivors, that was the first time that the brothers openly voiced their love for one another.

When he began to assure the company that he was all right — "I'm not losing it. I'm not going bananas." — it seemed clear that he was deteriorating, and the feeling grew that his death was near. He began calling for people — his wife, his brothers, his children and grandchildren — and as they appeared, he spoke repeatedly of his love for them. He asked for corn soup, for singing, for devotions, for coals from the still-smoldering tepee fire so he could burn cedar.

The message started to get around. People began to show up. A drum was tied with such speed that the following day it was judged to have set a record. Reuben was moved to his bedroom, and the closest in his family surrounded his bed. His son Darren would later report that what struck him first as he approached his father's bedside was that his eyes sparkled. Others in the living room and hallway got devotions going and lifted their voices in songs that Reuben kept insisting he wanted to hear.

Then, with extraordinary rapidity, the weather changed dramatically. From the cloudless day that it had been, clouds emerged, moving in so rapidly that within minutes the entire sky was covered. The air grew blacker by the second. Lightning flashed and thunder rolled — first at a distance, but suddenly it jumped to the inner side of the ridge that borders the reservation. The singing increased in intensity. Members of the immediate family had a quick huddle as to whether to take Reuben to the hospital, but he wouldn't hear of the idea. It was his last earthly decision.

Outdoors, the lightning and thunder escalated. "It wasn't like regular lightning," Norman later reported. "There was nothing in the east;

> it all came from the west. It didn't even seem like lightning — just
> blinding light, rushing at us from the west. Since then I have won-
> dered if I just saw it that way because of the state my mind was in,

for it definitely was in a state. Everything seemed to be happening at once — people coming and going in and out of the house. But it couldn't have just been my mental condition, because everybody saw the weather the way I did.

There was one climactic burst of light. It had to have been lightning, but it didn't look like lightning. It looked like a blinding white curtain unrolling from the sky right down to where we were standing, lighting up the whole reservation. It was after midnight — it must have been around one a.m. — but we could see everything as if it were broad daylight.

And then, right in the midst of all this commotion, I heard Cathy, Reuben's wife, give a war whoop and I knew at once that Reuben had died, for that's what some of us Indians do when a relative dies — give a war whoop. The crying began.

Some years before, at the funeral of a clan member, Reuben had said to his brother Norman, who was next to him in age, "The day when I leave, Cathy is going to give my body to you, but I want you to give it back to her." Thus it was Cathy, his wife, who took over and made the arrangements for the funeral.

Thinking back on Reuben's final day on earth, John had this to say:

Everyone experienced that day differently. For me, it was strange. It was as if Reuben was right there with us, yet he wasn't there. He was sitting there, but you could have walked right through him. Perhaps I had that feeling because his ego had already departed. As for me, I wasn't walking on the ground that day. I couldn't feel myself walking even when I was walking. I didn't know if I was tired. I didn't know if I was hungry. I was just going through the motions.

Fifteen months later, on Sunday, October 23, 1994, at Haskell Indian University in Lawrence, Kansas, a flag was raised as a permanent tribute to the life of Reuben Snake and his labors in behalf of the Native American Church.

Appendix

A Brief History of the Native American Church

Jay C. Fikes

Veneration of the small spineless cactus called peyote probably began immediately after the first hunter-gatherers discovered its remarkable effects. The Native American deification of the plant is estimated to be about 10,000 years old. Peyote cactus buttons uncovered in Shumla Cave in southern Texas have been radiocarbon dated to 5000 B.C. The Huichol Indians of northwestern Mexico still use peyote sacramentally. Their peyote pilgrimage may have been in place by 200 A.D. Scholars consider it the oldest sacramental use of peyote in North America.

Huichols revere Peyote as the heart, soul, and memory of their Creator, Deer-Person. Huichol healers and singers achieve such union with their Creator, as incarnated in Peyote, that Peyote speaks through them, as here:

If you come to know me intimately, you shall be like me and feel like I do. Although you may not see me, I shall always be your elder brother. I am called the flower of Deer-Person. Have no fear, for I shall always be the flower of God.[1]

Deer-Person, the supreme teacher of the Huichol, teaches songs, reveals himself to shamanic healers through his Peyote spirit, and punishes those who violate his moral precepts. "It is because of the wisdom of Deer-Person," we are told, "that shamans exist. That is how we Huichols are able to diagnose diseases with our visionary ability and soul, which are the eyes of Deer-Person. That is our method of curing."[2]

167

Huichol Peyote rituals have profound roots in the archaic hunter's view of the world. Huichols follow strict rules when they pilgrimage to collect their sacred plant in the high desert nearly 400 kilometers northeast of their homeland. They publicly confess their sexual transgressions and abstain from sex and salt. They testify that the Creator was destined to take the form of deer and Peyote. Because Peyote embodies the spirit, and is the heart of Deer-Person, they must hunt him with arrows. When they eat his heart, incarnated in the Peyote cactus, they eat it raw, honoring the precedent set by their elder brothers, the immortal wolves. To commemorate the wolves eating the deer raw,

> our Peyote hunters must do likewise when they eat his heart (Peyote). As the deer escaped from the ancestor-deities, he took the form of Peyote there in Huiricuta (the holyland where Peyote is collected). Peyote grows in clusters which resemble the shape of a deer. That is why we shoot it with our arrows.[3]

Huichol religion parallels Christianity in that the Creator, out of compassion for his people, subjects himself to the limitations of this world. In Christianity he incarnates himself as a man who dies but is resurrected to save human beings; in Huichol belief he dies and is reborn in the Peyote plant to give his people wisdom. The Aztec are the cultural cousins of the Huichol, and their word *peyotl* or *peyutl* denotes the pericardium, the envelope or covering of the heart. This corresponds strictly to the Huichol belief that Peyote embodies the Creator's heart.

From the very beginning, immigrants to the New World have misunderstood the Native American adoration of peyote. In 1620, sixty years after the sacramental use of peyote was first reported by the Franciscan Friar Sahagun, the Spanish Inquisition denounced it as diabolic and made its use illegal. Inquisitional persecution of Mexican Indian peyotists included torture and death.

We have many early, brief descriptions of peyote use among natives of northwestern Mexico, and two Inquisition reports from Santa Fe, New Mexico, which document peyote's use in divination, showing that by 1630 it was already being used five hundred miles north of its natural habitat. Serious study of its use, however, did not begin until the 1890s, when James Mooney, an anthropologist from the Smithsonian Institution, researched Peyote meetings among the Kiowa in Oklahoma. From there he went on to study Peyote rituals on other reservations as well as its use by the Tarahumara in Mexico. In 1918, after testifying in favor of Native American peyotists at Congressional hearings, Mooney advised peyotists of various Oklahoma tribes to obtain a legal charter to protect their religious freedom. With Mooney's help and encouragement, the Native American Church was officially incorporated in 1918.

The exact route and time of diffusion of what is today the Native American Church of North America is unclear. All available evidence suggests that the Carrizo culture, which once occupied the area that extends from Laredo to the Gulf of Mexico in what is now Texas, was instrumental in developing Peyote meetings among Native Americans who resided there. Carrizo Peyote rituals that were observed in 1649 included all-night dancing around a fire, but with no tepee. The western neighbors of the Carrizo, the Lipan Apache, seemed to have transformed the Carrizo ceremony before teaching it to the Kiowa, Kiowa-Apache, and Comanche.

Peyote was accepted as a remedy and inspiration by members of many Oklahoma tribes during an era of agonizing cultural disintegration, which reached a peak during the 1880s. By 1874, the Kiowa and Comanche, once proud warriors of the southern Plains, were confined to reservations in Oklahoma. The loss of liberty intrinsic to reservation life brought great pain and suffering to all Native Americans. Perhaps because it provided a powerful alternative to both ancient tribal religions and missionary-controlled versions of Christianity, the Peyote religion spread like wildfire. In the 1880s, two new religious movements were popular among Native Americans. One, the Ghost Dance, tried to renew the old ways. Following the Wounded Knee Massacre of 1890, the Ghost Dance practically disappeared. The other, the Peyote religion, allowed members to establish a new identity which combined aboriginal and Christian elements. Except for the secular pow-wow, Peyote meetings are now the most popular Native American gatherings.

The Peyote meeting is a genuinely intertribal institution. Reservations established in Indian territory, which subsequently became the State of Oklahoma, contained tribes that had formerly been scattered across the country. In the early 1880s, after the railroads reached Laredo, Texas, in the heart of the area where peyote is gathered, the stage was set for rapid communication between Oklahoma tribes and all other Native Americans. The railroads made it easier for Native Americans to obtain their sacrament and share their religious traditions.

The most famous of all Oklahoma peyotists was Quanah Parker, a Comanche, who helped bring Half Moon style Peyote meetings to members of the Delaware, Caddo, Cheyenne, Arapaho, Ponca, Oto, Pawnee, Osage, and other tribes. Half Moon meetings have remained freer of Christian infusions than have those of the Big Moon branch of the Church which a Caddo, John Wilson, pioneered in disseminating. By 1910, both of these styles of meetings had spread far beyond the Oklahoma reservations where they originated.

As soon as Christian missionaries became aware of the sacramental use of peyote on their reservations they began to agitate against it. First in Oklahoma and later elsewhere, Indian agents joined the missionaries in lobbying to outlaw the substance. The Indians bravely defended their religious freedom in their respective states and in Congress. One of the most eloquent of these defenders was Albert Hensley, a Winnebago educated at the Carlisle Indian School. By 1908, Hensley and the Winnebago had come to regard Peyote as both a Holy Medicine and a Christian sacrament. "To us it is a portion of the body of Christ," Hensley said, "even as the communion bread is believed to be a portion of Christ's body by other Christian denominations. Christ spoke of a Comforter who was to come. It never came to Indians until it was sent by God in the form of this Holy Medicine."[4]

Descriptions of still-existing Peyote rituals that are essentially free of Christian admixtures — those of the Tepehuan, Cora, Huichol, and Tarahumara tribes in Mexico, for example — hint of pre-Columbian origins of contemporary Church meetings, for anthropologists can point to aboriginal counterparts for virtually all of the sacred artifacts that the Native American Church uses. Sacramental smoking of tobacco wrapped in corn husks, the staff of authority, feather fans, gourd rattles, incense, a central fireplace, and emphasis on the four cardinal directions all have their parallels in Mexican Peyote rituals that continue today. Some features of Mexican Peyote rituals, however — outdoor dancing and elaborate ritual pilgrimages to collect peyote are examples — have disappeared or were diluted as Peyote meetings moved north into the Plains. Christian doctrine has gradually redefined the meaning of many ancient sacred artifacts. To cite a single instance, in Big Moon (also called Cross Fire) meetings where Christian infusions are most in evidence, sacred tobacco is no longer used as a catalyst for prayer; the Bible has replaced it. Despite such differences, the Cross Fire still shares a common ceremonial core with the Half Moon rituals.

Today the Native American Church of North America has eighty chapters and members belonging to some seventy Native American Nations. In the continental United States, every state west of the Mississippi has at least one chapter. The steady proliferation of its membership among diverse North American tribes has made it Native America's largest religious organization. Its total membership is estimated to be around 250,000.

Singing occupies about sixty percent of the Church's devotional ritual. Each of about twenty-five worshipers has ample opportunity to sing to the accompaniment of a gourd rattle and small drum that is pounded rapidly. Singing is often in the local Native American language, but English phrases like "Jesus only" and "He's the Savior" are likely to erupt. Worshipers sing, drum, pray, meditate, and consume peyote during all-night meetings. Most meetings are held for healing, baptism, funerals, and birthdays.

Peyote is regarded as a gift from God. It counters the crav-ing for alcohol and is not eaten to induce visions. It heals and teaches righteousness. It is eaten, or consumed as a tea, ac-cording to a formal ritual. Reverently, it is passed clockwise around the circle of church members a number of times in the course of all-night prayer vigils.

The Church has no professional, paid clergy. Members are free to interpret Bible passages according to their own under-standing. Morality is basically Christian and stresses the need to abstain from alcohol and be faithful to one's spouse. Other prominent values include truthfulness, fulfilling one's family obligations, economic self-sufficiency, praying for the sick, and praying for peace.

NOTES

1. Quoted in Jay C. Fikes, *Carlos Castaneda, Academic Opportunism, and the Psychedelic Sixties* (Victoria, B.C.: Millenia Press, 1993), 235.
2. *Ibid.*, 193.
3. *Ibid.*, 195.
4. Quoted in Omer C. Stewart, *Peyote Religion: A History* (Norman: University of Oklahoma Press, 1987), 157.

Contributors

Edward F. Anderson received his Ph.D. in botany from the Claremont Graduate School. Having taught at Pomona College and Whitman College, he is currently Senior Research Botanist at the Desert Botanical Garden in Phoenix. Parts of the present essay are excerpted from the second edition of his book, *Peyote: The Divine Cactus*, (Tucson: The University of Arizona Press, 1996).

James Botsford is the Director of the Indian Law Office of Wisconsin Judicare. He has represented the Native American Church in various legal matters throughout the past decade, and was one of the attorneys representing that Church in securing passage of the American Indian Religious Freedom Act Amendments of 1994, the text of which appears in Chapter Five of this book.

Phil Cousineau is writer and codirector of *The Peyote Road: Ancient Religion in Contemporary Crisis*, and author of several books, most recently, *Soul: An Archaeology*, and *Prayers at 3 A.M.*

Walter B. Echo-Hawk is a Pawnee Indian lawyer employed as a staff attorney for the Native American Rights Fund. He has specialized in First Amendment rights for Native peoples and, like Botsford, was active in securing passage of the bill previously referred to.

Jay C. Fikes, Ph.D., president of the Institute of Inter-Cultural Affairs, is listed in "Who's Who of Emerging Leaders." He is a consultant, educator, speaker, and advocate for Native Americans. Among his recent works is *Carlos Castaneda, Academic Opportunism, and the Psychedelic Sixties*, and a documentary film on the Huichol Indians.

Gary Rhine is producer and codirector of *The Peyote Road: Ancient Religion in Contemporary Crisis*. See page 10 for its availability.

Huston Smith — whose teaching in philosophy and world religions has spanned Washington University, the Massachusetts Institute of Technology, and Syracuse University — is currently visiting professor at the University of California, Berkeley. He is the author of eight books of which the best known is *The World's Religions*.

Reuben Snake is amply identified in the book itself.

We would also like to acknowledge the following people, whose contributions and spirit have made this book possible.

Loretta Afraid-of-Bear Cook
Joe American Horse
Elmer L. Blackbird
Tom Cook
Truman Dailey
Larry Etsitty
John Emhoola
Floyd Flores
Eva Gap
Albert Hensley
Lawrence Hunter
Bernard Ice
Andy Kozad
Ralph Kochampanaskin
Fidel Moreno
Francis Mesteth

Patricia Mousetrail Russell
Troy Nakai
Dewey Neconish
Old Crow
Quanah Parker
John Rave
Bernard Red Cloud
Willie Riggs, Sr.
Alfred Leo Smith
Ted Strong
Irvin Tachonie
Thomas Wayka
Beatrice Weasel Bear
Johnny White Cloud
Robert Billie White Horse
Paris Williams